LONDON'S GROWING UP!

NLA Insight Study

NLA, The Building Centre
26 Store Street
London WC1E 7BT

www.newlondonarchitecture.org/nlatallbuildings
#nlatallbuildings

This book is published by NLA to accompany the NLA exhibition London's Growing Up!

3 April — 12 June 2014

© NLA — London's Centre for the Built Environment

ISBN 978-0-9927189-1-6

CONTENTS

INTRODUCTION — 03

MAP
Location of future tall buildings in London — 04

CHAPTER 1:
What determines the scale and location of tall buildings? — 12

1.1 Densification
1.2 The Market
1.3 Controls and Policies
1.4 The Mayor and the London Plan
1.5 London View Management Framework
1.6 Secretary of State
1.7 Boroughs and Local Plan
1.8 The City of London
1.9 Southwark
1.10 City of Westminster
1.11 Section 106 and the Community Infrastructure Levy (CIL)
1.12 English Heritage
1.13 UNESCO
1.14 Right to Light
1.15 The Crown
1.16 Residents and Neighbourhood Plans

CHAPTER 2:
50 years of tall buildings in London — 36

2.1 Pre 1960s
2.2 Residential towers in the 1960s and 1970s
2.3 Commercial towers in the 1960s and 1970s
2.4 1980s and 1990s
2.5 2000s

CHAPTER 3:
The current wave of tall towers — 54

3.1 Numbers, height and status
3.2 Location
3.3 Type and use
3.4 Key findings
3.5 Public perceptions

CHAPTER 4:
Key areas of growth — 70

4.1 Vauxhall Nine Elms
4.2 Elephant and Castle
4.3 Blackfriars Road
4.4 Waterloo
4.5 Canary Wharf & Wood Wharf
4.6 Isle of Dogs & South Quay
4.7 City Fringe
4.8 City Road Basin
4.9 Stratford
4.10 Deptford, Lewisham and Greenwich
4.11 Croydon
4.12 White City and Earls Court
4.13 Brent Cross Cricklewood
4.14 Old Oak Common

CHAPTER 5:
London's future skyline — 102

REFERENCES — 108

PROFILES — 110

INTRODUCTION

This NLA Insight Study brings together a mass of data regarding planning applications for tall buildings that is available through the planning portals of local authorities, together with published and unpublished future plans for developments, in order to highlight some of the massive changes that are taking place in the capital over the next couple of decades.

As a result of the exponential growth in London's population, the Mayor and the boroughs have to deliver new homes at a scale not seen since the 1930s, but unlike the 1930s, covering great swathes of Metroland is no answer to our current problems. We need to conserve our land area just as we need to conserve all natural resources – and that means increasing densities.

While in theory increased density does not mean building tall buildings, it is only on large sites with a coherent masterplan that the full benefits of low to mid-rise high-density can be developed. In the sort of smaller, expensive sites generally found in the Central Activity Zone (CAZ), the pressure to build tall – in the present planning system – is hard to resist.

NLA believes that an open and informed debate about the pressures of housing a fast growing city, and the resulting solutions, is essential in the development of a better city. The scale of change revealed in this study will come as a surprise to many and we believe the debate that emerges will have a positive impact on the quality of buildings that will enhance our skyline in the future.

Canary Wharf

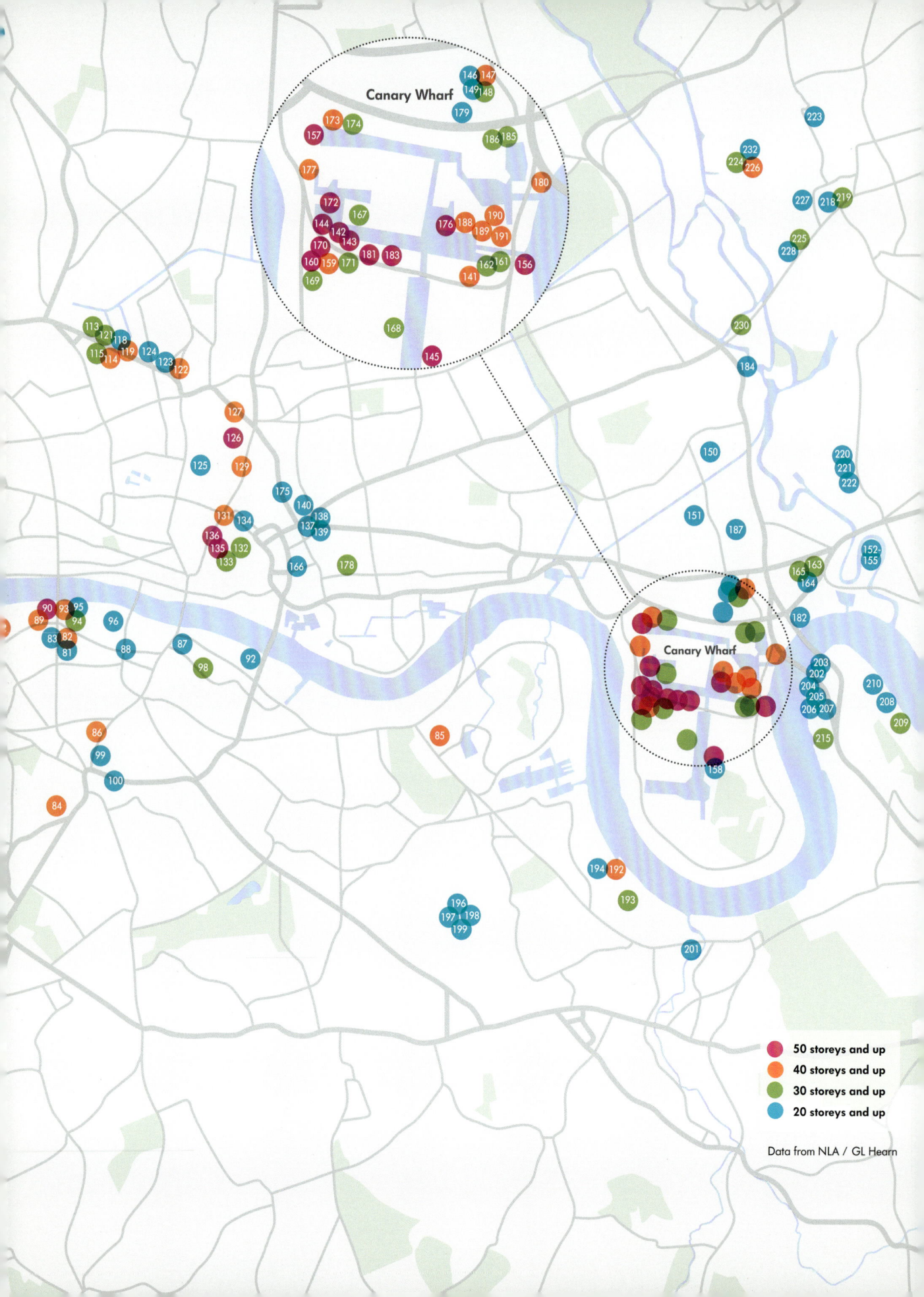

- ● 50 storeys and up
- ● 40 storeys and up
- ● 30 storeys and up
- ● 20 storeys and up

Data from NLA / GL Hearn

Nine Elms

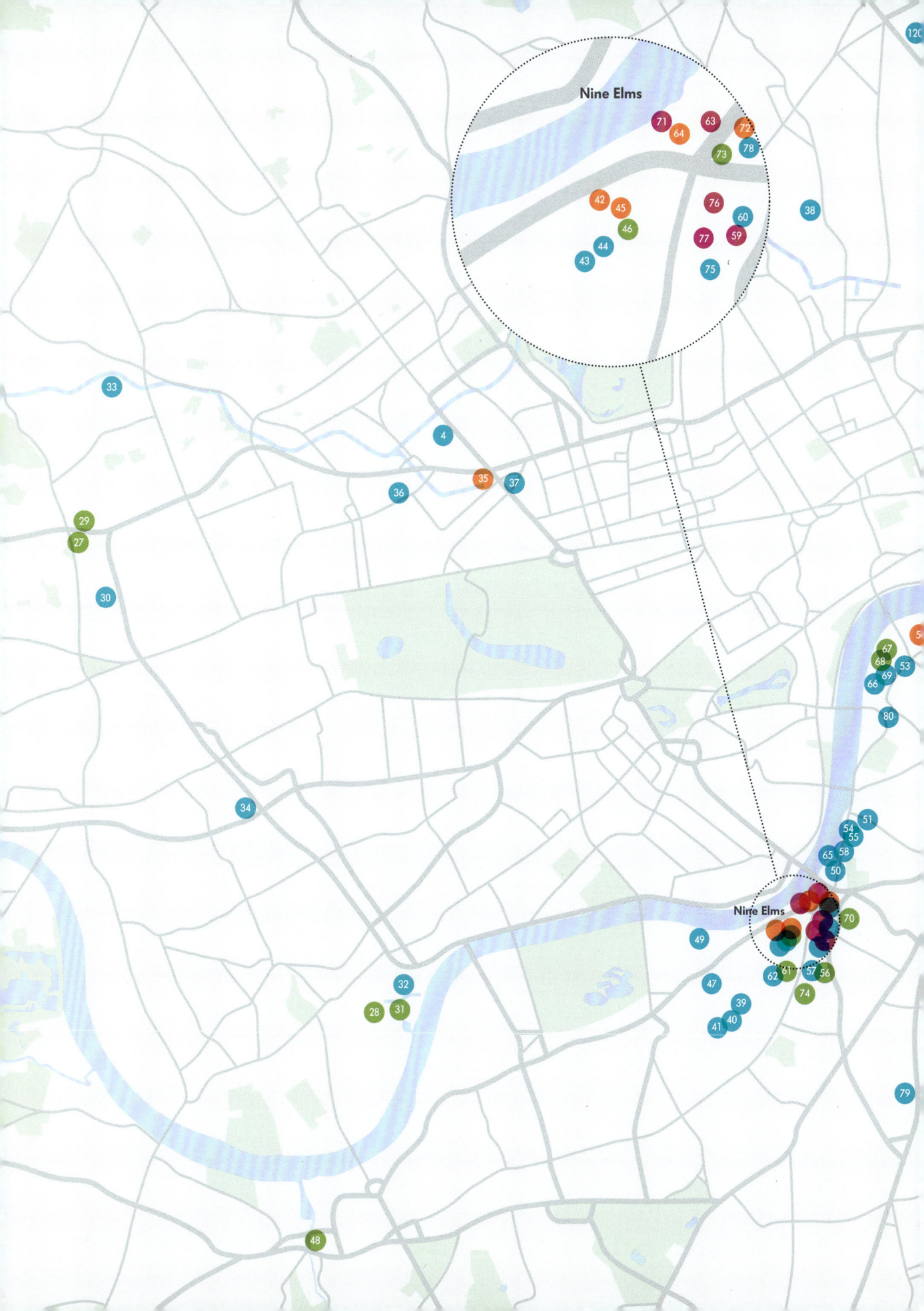

MAP
Location of future tall buildings in London

236 proposals for tall buildings over 20 storeys within Greater London, from research by GL Hearn for NLA

Project name
Borough
Architect
Developer
Height / Storeys
Type
Status

*indicates projects which fall outside the boundaries of the map

1
The Tower GWQ*
Hounslow TW8 0BW
Assael Architecture
Barratt West London
100m / 29 storeys
Mixed Use
Under construction

2
The Apex*
Ealing W5 2BS
Darling Associates Architecture
Frogmore Estates
76m / 21 storeys
-
Approved

3
Copeland School*
Brent HA9
GMH Rock Townsend
Copland Community School / Technology Centre Foundation
82m / 28 storeys
Residential & Retail
Approved

4
399 Edgware Road
Brent NW2
Sheppard Robson
Development Securities
72m / 22 storeys
Residential
Approved

5
Karma House*
Brent HA9 0UU
HTA
Donban
58m / 20 storeys
Residential
Approved

6
Wembley Plot W03*
Brent HA9
Rogers Stirk Harbour + Partners
Quintain Estates
85m / 25 storeys
Commercial
Approved

7
Brent Cross Market Quarter MQ1 (1)*
Barnet NW2
Allies and Morrison
B.X.C Development Partners
100m / 25 storeys
Commercial
Approved

8
Brent Cross Market Quarter MQ1 (2)*
Barnet NW2
Allies and Morrison
B.X.C Development Partners
65m / 21 storeys
Residential
Approved

9
Brent Cross West BXW1 (1)*
Barnet NW2
Allies and Morrison
B.X.C Development Partners
65m / 21 storeys
Residential
Approved

10
Brent Cross West BXW1 (2)*
Barnet NW2
Allies and Morrison
B.X.C Development Partners
65m / 21 storeys
Residential
Approved

11
Brent Cross West BXW2 (1)*
Barnet NW2
Allies and Morrison
B.X.C Development Partners
65m / 21 storeys
Residential
Approved

12
Brent Cross West BXW2 (2)*
Barnet NW2
Allies and Morrison
B.X.C Development Partners
65m / 21 storeys
Residential
Approved

13
Brent Terrace BT2 (1)*
Barnet NW2
Allies and Morrison
B.X.C Development Partners
65m / 21 storeys
Residential
Approved

14
Brent Terrace BT2 (2)*
Barnet NW2
Allies and Morrison
B.X.C Development Partners
65m / 21 storeys
Residential
Approved

15
Brent Terrace BT4 (1)*
Barnet NW2
Allies and Morrison
B.X.C Development Partners
65m / 21 storeys
Residential
Approved

16
Eastern Lands EL1 (1)*
Barnet NW2
Allies and Morrison
B.X.C Development Partners
65m / 21 storeys
Residential
Approved

17
Eastern Lands EL1 (2)*
Barnet NW2
Allies and Morrison
B.X.C Development Partners
65m / 21 storeys
Residential
Approved

18
Eastern Lands EL3 (1)*
Barnet NW2
Allies and Morrison
B.X.C Development Partners
65m / 21 storeys
Residential
Approved

19
Eastern Lands EL3 (2)*
Barnet NW2
Allies and Morrison
B.X.C Development Partners
65m / 21 storeys
Residential
Approved

20
Eastern Lands EL4 (1)*
Barnet NW2
Allies and Morrison
B.X.C Development Partners
65m / 21 storeys
Residential
Approved

21
Station Quarter SQ1 (1)*
Barnet NW2
Allies and Morrison
B.X.C Development Partners
100m / 25 storeys
Commercial
Approved

22
Station Quarter SQ1 (2)*
Barnet NW2
Allies and Morrison
B.X.C Development Partners
100m / 25 storeys
Commercial
Approved

23
Station Quarter SQ1 (3)*
Barnet NW2
Allies and Morrison
B.X.C Development Partners
100m / 25 storeys
Residential
Approved

24
Station Quarter SQ2 (1)*
Barnet NW2
Allies and Morrison
B.X.C Development Partners
100m / 25 storeys
Commercial
Approved

25
Station Quarter SQ2 (2)*
Barnet NW2
Allies and Morrison
B.X.C Development Partners
100m / 25 storeys
Commercial
Approved

26
West Hendon Estate (Block E2)*
Barnet W9
Allies and Morrison
Barratt Metropolitan
85m / 27 storeys
Residential
Approved

27
Brickfields (Block J)
Hammersmith & Fulham W12
Eric Parry Architects
Helical Bar / Aviva Investors
108m / 32 storeys
Residential & Retail
Approved

28
Chelsea Creek Tower
Hammersmith & Fulham SW10
Broadway Maylan
St George
86m / 30 storeys
Residential & Retail
Approved

29
Imperial West Tower
Hammersmith & Fulham W12
PLP Architecture
Imperial College London
105m / 35 storeys
University
Approved

30
Westfield Tower,
Ariel Way
Hammersmith & Fulham W12
Allies and Morrison
Westfield Shoppingtowns Limited
23 storeys
Residential & Commercial
Proposed

31
Chelsea Waterfront,
Lots Road Tower 1
Kensington and Chelsea / Hammersmith and Fulham SW10
Farrells
Hutchison Whampoa Properties
130m / 37 storeys
Residential
Under construction

32
Chelsea Waterfront,
Lots Road Tower 2
Kensington and Chelsea / Hammersmith and Fulham SW10
Farrells
Hutchison Whampoa Properties
92m / 25 storeys
Residential
Under construction

33
Ladbroke Green
Kensington and Chelsea
W10
CZWG Architects
Peabody Trust
67m / 22 storeys
Residential & Commercial
Proposed

34
100 West Cromwell Road
Kensington and Chelsea
SW5
Benson + Forsyth
Spen Hill Developments
82m / 24 storeys
Residential & Retail
Proposed

35
1 Merchant Square
Westminster W2 1JU
Robin Partington Architects
European Land Partnership Ltd
140m / 42 storeys
Residential & Hotel
Approved

36
Paddington Triangle
Westminster W2 6BA
Grimshaw Architects
Crossrail
21 storeys
Commercial & Retail
Proposed

37
West End Green
Westminster W2 1DH
Squire and Partners
West End Green Property Ltd
85m / 22 storeys
Residential
Under construction

38
Maiden Lane
Camden NW1 9YS
PRP Architects
LB Camden
66m / 20 storeys
Residential
Approved

39
New Covent Garden Market (Apex Site - A1)
Wandsworth SW8 5NX
Skidmore Owing & Merrill
VSM (NCGM) Ltd
86m / 26 storeys
Residential
Proposed

40
New Covent Garden Market (Apex Site - A2)
Wandsworth SW8 5NX
Skidmore Owing & Merrill
VSM (NCGM) Ltd
80m / 23 storeys
Residential
Proposed

41
New Covent Garden Market (Apex Site - A4)
Wandsworth SW8 5NX
Skidmore Owing & Merrill
VSM (NCGM) Ltd
77m / 23 storeys
Residential
Proposed

42
New Covent Garden Market (Northern Site - N1)
Wandsworth SW8 5NX
Skidmore Owing & Merrill
VSM (NCGM) Ltd
154m / 46 storeys
Residential
Proposed

43
New Covent Garden Market (Northern Site - N6)
Wandsworth SW8 5NX
Skidmore Owing & Merrill
VSM (NCGM) Ltd
84m / 24 storeys
Residential
Proposed

44
New Covent Garden Market (Northern Site - N7)
Wandsworth SW8 5NX
Skidmore Owing & Merrill
VSM (NCGM) Ltd
104m / 29 storeys
Residential & Commercial
Proposed

45
New Covent Garden Market (Northern Site – N8)
Wandsworth SW8 5NX
Skidmore Owing & Merrill
VSM (NCGM) Ltd
180m / 54 storeys
Residential
Proposed

46
New Covent Garden Market (Northern Site – N9)
Wandsworth SW8 5NX
Skidmore Owing & Merrill
VSM (NCGM) Ltd
122m / 36 storeys
Residential
Proposed

47
Nine Elms Parkside Tower
Wandsworth SW8
Allies and Morrison
Royal Mail Group
80m / 23 storeys
Mixed Use
Approved

48
Ram Brewery
Wandsworth SW18 4LB
EPR Architects
Greenland Holdings Group
115m / 36 storeys
Residential & Retail
Approved

49
Riverlight
Wandsworth SW8
Rogers Stirk Harbour + Partners
St James Group
21 storeys
Residential & Mixed Use
Under construction

50
36-48 Albert Embankment
Lambeth SE1
Make Architects
OKTIS Holdings
75m / 23 storeys
Residential & Commercial
Proposed

51
81 Black Prince Road
Lambeth SE1 7SZ
Keith Williams Architects
Ristoia Ltd
73m / 23 storeys
Commercial & Residential
Under construction

52
Doon Street Tower
Lambeth SE1
Lifschutz Davidson Sandilands
Coin Street Community Builders
140m / 43 storeys
Residential & Mixed Use
Approved

53
Elizabeth House
Lambeth SE1
David Chipperfield Architects
London & Regional / Chelsfield PLC
94m / 22 storeys
Commercial & Residential
Approved

54
Hampton House
(Building 1),
20 Albert Embankment
Lambeth SW8
Foster + Partners
St James Group
85m / 27 storeys
Residential & Retail
Approved

55
Hampton House
(Building 2),
20 Albert Embankment
Lambeth SW8
Foster + Partners
St James Group
76m / 24 storeys
Residential & Retail
Approved

56
Keybridge House
(Building A)
Lambeth SW8 1RG
Allies and Morrison
British Telecommunications PLC
133m / 36 storeys
Residential & Commercial
Proposed

57
Keybridge House
(Building F)
Lambeth SW8 1RG
Allies and Morrison
British Telecommunications PLC
77m / 22 storeys
Residential & Commercial
Proposed

58
Merano, 30-34 Albert Embankment
Lambeth SE1
Rogers Stirk Harbour + Partners
St James Group
86m / 28 storeys
Mixed Use
Under construction

59
New Bondway (Tower 1)
Lambeth SW8 1SQ
Kohn Pedersen Fox Associates/Tavernor
McLaren Property
50 storeys
Residential & Commercial
Proposed

60
New Bondway (Tower 2)
Lambeth SW8 1SQ
Kohn Pedersen Fox Associates/Tavernor
McLaren Property
24 storeys
Residential & Commercial
Proposed

61
Nine Elms Sainsburys
(Tower G)
Lambeth SW8 2LF
Rolfe Judd Architects
Sainsbury's Supermarket Ltd
129m / 37 storeys
Residential
Approved

62
Nine Elms Sainsburys
(Tower K)
Lambeth SW8 2LF
Rolfe Judd Architects
Sainsbury's Supermarket Ltd
90m / 29 storeys
Residential
Approved

63
One Nine Elms,
City Tower
Lambeth SW8 5NQ
Kohn Pedersen Fox Associates
Green Property Ltd / CIT Group
200m / 58 storeys
Residential & Commercial
Approved

64
One Nine Elms, River Tower
Lambeth SW8 5NQ
Kohn Pedersen Fox Associates
Green Property Ltd / CIT Group
161m / 43 storeys
Residential & Hotel
Approved

65
Prince Consort House,
27-29 Albert Embankment
Lambeth SE1
David Walker Architects
Jones Lang LaSalle
87m / 27 storeys
Residential & Retail
Proposed

66
Shell Centre (Building B3)
Lambeth SE1
Squire and Partners
Canary Wharf Group Plc
85m / 28 storeys
Residential & Retail
Proposed

67
Shell Centre (Building B4A)
Lambeth SE1
Squire and Partners
Canary Wharf Group Plc
113m / 37 storeys
Residential & Retail
Proposed

68
Shell Centre (Building B4B)
Lambeth SE1
Squire and Partners
Canary Wharf Group Plc
91m / 30 storeys
Residential & Retail
Proposed

69
Shell Centre (Building B6)
Lambeth SE1
Squire and Partners
Canary Wharf Group Plc
64m / 21 storeys
Residential & Retail
Proposed

70
30-60 South Lambeth Road
Lambeth SW8
Feilden Clegg Bradley Studios
Downing Developments
97m / 32 storeys
Residential
Under construction

71
The Tower, One St George Wharf
Lambeth SW8 2LE
Broadway Maylan
St George South London
181m / 53 storeys
Residential
Under construction

72
Vauxhall Cross Island (Tower 1)
Lambeth SW8 1SJ
Squire and Partners
Kylun Ltd
140m / 41 storeys
Residential
Approved

73
Vauxhall Cross Island (Tower 2)
Lambeth SW8 1SJ
Squire and Partners
Kylun Ltd
106m / 31 storeys
Residential
Approved

74
Vauxhall Sky Gardens
Lambeth SE1
Carey Jones Architects
Fraser Property Development UK
120m / 36 storeys
Residential & Commercial
Proposed

75
Vauxhall Square (Miles Street South)
Lambeth SW8
Allies and Morrison
CLS Holdings
87m / 26 storeys
Residential & Retail
Approved

76
Vauxhall Square (North)
Lambeth SW8
Allies and Morrison
CLS Holdings
168m / 50 storeys
Residential & Retail
Approved

77
Vauxhall Square (South)
Lambeth SW8
Allies and Morrison
CLS Holdings
168m / 50 storeys
Residential & Retail
Approved

78
Vauxhall Square (Wendle Court)
Lambeth SW8
Allies and Morrison
CLS Holdings
69m / 21 storeys
Residential & Retail
Approved

79
Wayland House
Lambeth SW9
PRP Architects
Network Housing Group
69m / 20 storeys
Residential
Under construction

80
199 Westminster Bridge Road
Lambeth SE1
Allford Hall Monaghan Morris
Urbanest
63m / 21 storeys
Residential & University
Under construction

81
20 Blackfriars Road (Office Tower)
Southwark SE1
Wilkinson Eyre Architects
Circleplane
109m / 23 storeys
Commercial
Approved

82
20 Blackfriars Road (Residential Tower)
Southwark SE1
Wilkinson Eyre Architects
Circleplane
148m / 42 storeys
Residential & Retail
Approved

83
240 Blackfriars Road
Southwark SE1 9UF
AHMM
Great Ropemaker Partnership (Great Portland Estates + BP Pension Fund)
85m / 20 storeys
Commercial
Under construction

84
360 London, Newington Butts
Southwark SE11 4QU
Rogers Stirk Harbour + Partners
Mace / Essential Living
147m / 45 storeys
Mixed Use
Approved

85
Decathlon
Southwark
Maccreanor Lavington / David Chipperfield
Sellar
40 storeys
Residential & Mixed use
Proposed

86
Eileen House, 80-94 Newington Causeway
Southwark SE1 6BN
Allies and Morrison
Merryvale No.6 International
125m / 41 storeys
Residential
Under construction

87
Fielden House
Southwark
Renzo Piano Building workshop
Sellar
27 storeys
Residential
Proposed

88
Gagarin Tower, 55 Southwark Street
Southwark SE1
Studio 44
Henry George Ltd
84m / 25 storeys
Residential
Proposed

89
King's Reach Tower
Southwark SE1 9LS
Kohn Pedersen Fox Associates
King's Reach Estates Ltd / CIT Real Estate LLP
155m / 41 storeys
Mixed Use
Under construction

90
One Blackfriars
Southwark SE1 9UF
Ian Simpson Architects
St George South London
170m / 50 storeys
Residential & Hotel
Under construction

91
One The Elephant
Southwark SE1 6SQ
Squire and Partners
Lend Lease
127m / 37 storeys
Residential & Retail
Under construction

92
One Tower Bridge (Block 5)
Southwark SE1
Squire and Partners
Berkeley Homes PLC
75m / 21 storeys
Residential
Under Construction

93
Sampson House and Ludgate House (Ludgate B)
Southwark SE1
PLP Architecture
The Carlyle Group
170m / 48 storeys
Mixed Use & Retail
Proposed

94
Sampson House and Ludgate House (Sampson House B)
Southwark SE1
PLP Architecture
The Carlyle Group
112m / 31 storeys
Mixed Use & Retail
Proposed

95
Sampson House and Ludgate House (Sampson House C)
Southwark SE1
PLP Architecture
The Carlyle Group
98m / 27 storeys
Mixed Use & Retail
Proposed

96
South Bank Tower, 185 Park Street
Southwark SE1
Squire + Partners
Delancey
75m / 23 storeys
Residential & Mixed use
Proposed

97
The Blades*
Southwark
Assael Architecture
Ministry of Sound
41 storeys
Residential
Proposed

98
The Quill
Southwark SE1 3QD
SPPARC Architecture
Kings College London / Investream
109m / 31 storeys
Residential & Retail
Approved

99
The Signal Building
Southwark SE1 6BN
Allies and Morrison
Neobrand
70m / 22 storeys
Residential & Commercial
Approved

100
Tribeca Square
Southwark SE1
PKS Architects
Oakmayne Properties / Delancey
76m / 23 storeys
Residential & Hotel
Under construction

101
Addiscombe Road*
Croydon CR0 6SE
Allies and Morrison
Royal Mail
21 storeys
Residential
Approved

102
Croydon College*
Croydon CR0
Darling Associates
Pheonix Logistics / Croydon College
37 storeys
Hotel & Residential
Proposed

07

103
4-20 Edridge Road*
Croydon CR0
MDR Associates
Edridge BV
70m / 23 storeys
Residential & Commercial
Proposed

104
Morello Tower*
Croydon CR0
Make Architects
Menta
171m / 55 storeys
Residential & Retail
Approved

105
One Lansdowne Road*
Croydon CR9 1LL
CZWG Architects
Guildhouse-Rosepride
199m / 51 storeys
Residential & Commercial
Approved

106
Ruskin Square Phase 1*
Croydon CR0
AHMM
Places for People
68m / 22 storeys
Residential
Under Construction

107
Ruskin Square,
Croydon R03*
Croydon CR7
Foster + Partners & AHMM
Stanhope and Schroders
67m / 20 storeys
Residential
Approved

108
St George's House,
Park Lane*
Croydon CR9 1NR
EPR Architects
Legal & General
95m / 24 storeys
Residential & Commerical
Approved

109
Taberner House & The Queens Gardens*
Croydon CR9 3JS
Make Architects
Croydon Council Urban Regeneration Vehicle (CCURV) / Essential Living
179m / 32 storeys
Residential & Retail
Proposed

110
The Tower at Saffron Square*
Croydon CR0
Rolfe Judd Architects
Berkeley Homes PLC
131m / 43 storeys
Residential & Retail
Under construction

111
Brook House,
Cannon Rubber Factory,
881 High Road*
Haringey N17 8EY
KSS
Newton Housing Trust
22 storeys
Residential & Mixed Use
Approved

112
Hale Village*
Haringey N17
Flanagan Lawrence
Lee Valley Estates
82m / 25 storeys
Residential & Retail
Proposed

113
Canaletto, 257 City Road
Islington EC1V 1AD
UNStudio
Groveworld
100m / 31 storeys
Residential
Under construction

114
City Forum (Tower 1)
Islington EC1V 2PU
Foster + Partners
Berkeley Homes Plc
155m / 42 storeys
Residential & Retail
Proposed

115
City Forum (Tower 2)
Islington EC1V 2PU
Foster + Partners
Berkeley Homes Plc
137m / 36 storeys
Residential & Retail
Proposed

116
City North (Tower 1)*
Islington N4
Benson + Forsyth
United House
64m / 21 storeys
Residential & Retail
Under construction

117
City North (Tower 2)*
Islington N4
Benson + Forsyth
United House
64m / 21 storeys
Residential & Retail
Under construction

118
250 City Road (Tower 1)
Islington EC1V
BUJ Architects
Land Securities PLC
85m / 28 storeys
Residential & Retail
Approved

119
250 City Road (Tower 2)
Islington EC1V 2QZ
Foster + Partners
Berkeley Group
155m / 42 storeys
Residential
Proposed

120
Hornsey Road Arches
Islington N7
CZWG Architects
Ashburton Trading Ltd
78m / 25 storeys
Residential & Retail
Proposed

121
Lexicon, 261 City Road
Islington EC1
Skidmore Owing & Merrill
Mount Anvill
138m / 36 storeys
Residential
Under construction

122
145 City Road
Residential Building
Hackney N1 6AZ
Make Architects
Rocket Investments
134m / 40 storeys
Residential & Retail
Approved

123
151 City Road
Hackney EC1V 1JH
Squire and Partners
Endora Holdings Ltd
73m / 24 storeys
Hotel & Commercial
Under construction

124
Eagle House
Hackney EC1V 1NR
Farrells
Mount Anvill
82m / 26 storeys
Residential
Under construction

125
One Crown Place
Hackney EC2M 2PS
Kohn Pedersen Fox Associates
AlloyMtd Group
114m / 24 storeys
Commercial & Retail
Approved

126
Principal Place
Hackney N1
Foster + Partners
Brookfield
161m / 51 storeys
Residential & Retail
Approved

127
The Stage Shoreditch
Hackney EC2A
Pringle Brandon Perkins+Will
Plough Yard Developments
140m / 40 storeys
Residential & Retail
Approved

128
Woodberry Down*
Hackney N4
Fletcher Priest / Rolfe Judd
Berkeley Homes
30 storeys
Residential & Mixed use
Approved

129
100 Bishopsgate
City of London EC3
AMWB
100 Bishopsgate Partnership
172m / 40 storeys
Mixed Use
Proposed

130
20 Fenchurch Street
City of London EC3P 3DP
Rafael Viñoly Architects
Canary Wharf Group / Land Securities PLC
155m / 37 storeys
Commercial & Retail
Under construction

131
Four Seasons Hotel and Residences at Heron Plaza
City of London EC3
PLP Architecture
Heron International PLP
159m / 44 storeys
Hotel & Residential
Approved

132
40 Leadenhall Street
City of London EC3
Make Architects
Henderson
170m / 34 storeys
Mixed Use
Approved

133
52 Lime Street
City of London EC3M 7QD
Kohn Pedersen Fox Associates
WRBC Development UK Ltd
190m / 38 storeys
Commercial
Approved

134
60-70 St Mary Axe
City of London EC3A 8JQ
Foggo Associates
Targetfollow
90m / 22 storeys
Commercial
Approved

135
The Leadenhall Building
City of London EC3V 4AB
Rogers Stirk Harbour + Partners
British Land / Oxford Properties
224m / 52 storeys
Commercial & Retail
Under construction

136
The Pinnacle
City of London EC2N
Kohn Pedersen Fox Associates
Arab Investments
288m / 60 storeys
Commercial & Retail
Under construction

137
Aldgate Place (Tower 1)
Tower Hamlets E1 7PH
Allies and Morrison
Barratt London / British Land
82m / 21 storeys
Residential & Retail
Under construction

138
Aldgate Place (Tower 2)
Tower Hamlets E1 7PH
Allies and Morrison
Barratt London / British Land
24 storeys
Residential & Retail
Under construction

139
Aldgate Place (Tower 3)
Tower Hamlets E1 7PH
Allies and Morrison
Barratt London / British Land
25 storeys
Residential & Retail
Under construction

140
Altitude
Tower Hamlets E1
BFLS
Barratt Homes / Inoder
81m / 25 storeys
Residential & Retail
Under construction

141
Angel House,
225 Marsh Wall
Tower Hamlets E14
Jacobs Webber
The Angel Group
132m / 43 storeys
Residential & Commercial
Approved

142
Arrowhead Quay
(Tower 1)
Tower Hamlets E14
Glenn Howells Architects
Ballymore Properties
169m / 50 storeys
Residential & Retail
Proposed

143
Arrowhead Quay
(Tower 2)
Tower Hamlets E14
Glenn Howells Architects
Ballymore Properties
55 storeys
Residential
Proposed

144
Arrowhead Quay
(East Tower)
Tower Hamlets E14
Glenn Howells Architects
Ballymore Properties
182m / 55 storeys
Residential & Retail
Proposed

145
Baltimore Tower
Tower Hamlets E14
Skidmore Owing & Merrill
Frogmore / Galliard Homes
150m / 45 storeys
Residential & Retail
Under construction

146
Blackwall Reach
(Building H)
Tower Hamlets E14 0EW
Metropolitan Workshop and Jestico & Whiles
Swan Housing Association and Countryside Properties
25 storeys
Residential
Approved

147
Blackwall Reach
(Building I)
Tower Hamlets E14 0EW
Metropolitan Workshop and Jestico & Whiles
Swan Housing Association and Countryside Properties
40 storeys
Residential
Approved

148
Blackwall Reach
(Building K)
Tower Hamlets E14 0EW
Metropolitan Workshop and Jestico & Whiles
Swan Housing Association and Countryside Properties
35 storeys
Residential
Approved

149
Blackwall Reach
(Building M)
Tower Hamlets E14
Metropolitan Workshop and Jestico & Whiles
Swan Housing Association and Countryside Properties
63m / 20 storeys
Residential & Retail
Under construction

150
Bow Enterprise Park,
Cranwell Close
Tower Hamlets E3 3QY
ORMS Architecture and Design
Workspace Group
21 storeys
Residential & Mixed Use
Approved

151
Carmen Street
Tower Hamlets E14
Stock Woolstencroft Architects
Ballymore Properties
77m / 22 storeys
Residential & Retail
Approved

152
City Island (Building B),
Leamouth Peninsula
Tower Hamlets E14
Glenn Howells Architects
Ballymore Group
74m / 24 storeys
Residential & Retail
Under construction

153
City Island (Building C),
Leamouth Peninsula
Tower Hamlets E14
Glenn Howells Architects
Ballymore Group
79m / 26 storeys
Residential & Retail
Under construction

154
City Island (Building D),
Leamouth Peninsula
Tower Hamlets E14
Glenn Howells Architects
Ballymore Group
76m / 25 storeys
Residential & Retail
Under construction

155
City Island (Building EG),
Leamouth Peninsula
Tower Hamlets E14
Glenn Howells Architects
Ballymore Group
63m / 20 storeys
Residential & Retail
Under construction

156
City Pride
Tower Hamlets E14
Squire and Partners
Chalegrove Properties
239m / 75 storeys
Residential & Retail
Approved

157
Columbus Tower
(Hertsmere)
Tower Hamlets E14 4AB
-
Ryan Corporation (UK)
242m / 75 storeys
Residential & Hotel
Approved

158
Crossharbour District Centre (Building B)
Tower Hamlets E14 3BT
Broadway Malyan
Ashbourne Beech
71m / 23 storeys
Residential & Retail
Proposed

159
Cuba Street (Tower 1)
Tower Hamlets E14
3D Reid / Gultekin Architecture
Agaoglu Group
122m / 40 storeys
Hotel
Status Unknown

160
Cuba Street (Tower 2)
Tower Hamlets E14
3D Reid / Gultekin Architecture
Agaoglu Group
157m / 57 storeys
Hotel
Status Unknown

161
Dollar Bay
Tower Hamlets E14 9YJ
Ian Simpson Architects
Mount Anvil
115m / 31 storeys
Residential & Retail
Approved

162
1-18 Dollar Bay Court
Tower Hamlets E14 9YJ
Ian Simpson Architects
Mount Anvil
115m / 31 storeys
Residential & Commercial
Approved

163
East India Dock Road
(Block A)
Tower Hamlets E14
CZWG Architects
Barratt Homes
94m / 38 storeys
Residential
Status Unknown

164
East India Dock Road
(Block B)
Tower Hamlets E14
CZWG Architects
Barratt Homes
54m / 21 storeys
Residential
Status Unknown

165
East India Dock Road
(Block I)
Tower Hamlets E14
CZWG Architects
Barratt Homes
92m / 34 storeys
Residential
Status Unknown

166
Goodman's Fields
Tower Hamlets E1
Lifschutz Davidson Sandilands
Berkeley Homes
73m / 21 storeys
Residential
Under construction

167
Heron Quays West
Tower Hamlets E14
Adamson Associates
Canary Wharf Group
190m / 33 storeys
Commercial & Retail
Approved

168
Indescon Court Phase 2
Tower Hamlets E14
BFLS
Oracle
95m / 32 storeys
Residential & Hotel
Approved

169
Manilla Street
Tower Hamlets E14 8GB
Dexter Moren Architects
Ardmore Group
82m / 30 storeys
Mixed Use
Proposed

170
30 Marsh Wall
Tower Hamlets E14
21st Architecture
3DMW
53 storeys
Mixed Use
Approved

171
40 Marsh Wall
Tower Hamlets E14
BUJ Architects
Accor
128m / 39 storeys
Hotel & Retail
Approved

172
Newfoundland
Tower Hamlets E14
Horden Cherry Lee Architects
Canary Wharf Group
220m / 60 storeys
Residential
Proposed

173
North Quay (Tower 1)
Tower Hamlets E14
Pelli Clarke Pelli Architects
Canary Wharf Group Plc
216m / 44 storeys
Commercial
Approved

174
North Quay (Tower 3)
Tower Hamlets E14
Pelli Clarke Pelli Architects
Canary Wharf Group Plc
203m / 38 storeys
Commercial
Approved

175
One Commercial Street
Tower Hamlets E1
Broadway Maylan / John
Seifert Architects Ltd
Redrow Homes / Julius
Properties
79m / 23 storeys
Commercial & Residential
Under construction

176
One Wood Wharf
Tower Hamlets E14 9SB
Herzog & de Meuron
Canary Wharf Group
211.5m / 40+ storeys
Residential
Proposed

177
1 Park Place
Tower Hamlets E14
Horden Cherry Lea
Architects
Canary Wharf Group Plc
200m / 45 storeys
Commercial
Approved

178
Pinchin Street Tower
Tower Hamlets E1
HTA Architects
The Environment Trust
98m / 32 storeys
Residential & Retail
Status Unknown

179
Poplar Business Park,
Prestons Road (Block C)
Tower Hamlets E14 9RL
Barton Wilmore
Workspace Group PLC
22 storeys
Residential & Hotel
Approved

180
Providence Tower
Tower Hamlets E14
Skidmore Owing & Merrill
Ballymore Properties
136m / 44 storeys
Residential
Under construction

181
Quay House,
2 Admirals Way
Tower Hamlets E14
Kohn Pedersen Fox
Associates
Investin
75 storeys
Residential
Proposed

182
Reuters, Blackwall Yard
(Block A)
Tower Hamlets E14
Squire and Partners
Blaxmill Ltd
98m / 29 storeys
Residential
Approved

183
South Quay Plaza
Tower Hamlets E14
Foster + Partners
Berkeley Homes Plc
249m / 75 storeys
Residential
Proposed

184
Tesco Bromley by Bow
Tower Hamlets E3
Collado Collins
Tesco Stores Ltd
70m / 23 storeys
Residential & Hotel
Approved

185
Trafalgar Way (Tower 1)
Tower Hamlets E14
Darling Associates
Essential Living
122m / 36 storeys
Residential & Retail
Proposed

186
Trafalgar Way (Tower 2)
Tower Hamlets E14
Darling Associates
Essential Living
127m / 35 storeys
Residential & Hotel
Proposed

187
Willis Street Tower
Tower Hamlets E14
PRP Architects
Poplar HARCA
80m / 20 storeys
Residential & Commercial
Approved

188
A3 Wood Wharf
Tower Hamlets
Stanton Williams
Canary Wharf Group
157m / 42 storeys
Residential
Proposed

189
Wood Wharf 1
Tower Hamlets
Allies and Morrison
Canary Wharf Group
up to 211m / 40+ storeys
Commercial
Proposed

190
Wood Wharf 2
Tower Hamlets
Allies and Morrison
Canary Wharf Group
up to 211m / 40+ storeys
Commercial
Proposed

191
Wood Wharf 3
Tower Hamlets
Allies and Morrison
Canary Wharf Group
up to 211m / 40+ storeys
Commercial
Proposed

192
Convoys Wharf (Tower 1)
Lewisham SE8
Farrells
Hutchinson Whampoa
48 storeys
Residential
Proposed

193
Convoys Wharf (Tower 2)
Lewisham SE8
Farrells
Hutchinson Whampoa
91m / 32 storeys
Residential
Proposed

194
Convoys Wharf (Tower 3)
Lewisham SE8
Farrells
Hutchinson Whampoa
72m / 26 storeys
Residential
Proposed

195
Lewisham Gateway*
Lewisham SE13
PRP Architects
Muse Developments
77m / 22 storeys
Mixed Use
Approved

196
Surrey Canal Triangle -
Bolina North (Building 1)
Lewisham SE15 1EP
Studio Egret West / Sew
/ Townshend Landscape
Architects
Renewal
22 storeys
Residential & Retail
Approved

197
Surrey Canal Triangle
- Local Landmark Building
(Building 2)
Lewisham SE15 1EP
Studio Egret West / Sew
/ Townshend Landscape
Architects
Renewal
86m / 27 storeys
Residential & Commercial
Approved

198
Surrey Canal Triangle -
Stadium Avenue Marker
Building 1 (Building 3)
Lewisham SE15 1EP
Studio Egret West / Sew
/ Townshend Landscape
Architects
Renewal
21 storeys
Residential & Retail
Approved

199
Surrey Canal Triangle -
Stadium Avenue Marker
Building 2 (Building 4)
Lewisham SE15 1EP
Studio Egret West / Sew
/ Townshend Landscape
Architects
Renewal
21 storeys
Residential & Retail
Approved

200
Callis Yard Site*
Greenwich
Metropolis PD
Inland Homes
20 storeys
Residential
Proposed

201
Creekside Village East
(Block 2)
Greenwich SE8
Squire and Partners
Ampurius NuHomes
Investments Ltd
70m / 23 storeys
Residential
Approved

202
Greenwich Hotel
Greenwich SE10
Lifschutz Davidson
Sandilands
Queensgate Investments
and Arora Hotels
71m / 22 storeys
Hotel & Retail
Approved

203
Greenwich Hotel,
Apartments
Greenwich SE10
Lifschutz Davidson
Sandilands
Queensgate Investments
and Arora Hotels
81m / 24 storeys
Residential
Approved

204
**Greenwich Peninsula
Riverside** (1)
Greenwich SE10
Aukett Swanke
Knight Dragon
20+ storeys
Residential
Proposed

205
**Greenwich Peninsula
Riverside** (2)
Greenwich SE10
Aukett Swanke
Knight Dragon
20+ storeys
Residential
Proposed

206
**Greenwich Peninsula
Riverside** (3)
Greenwich SE10
Aukett Swanke
Knight Dragon
20+ storeys
Residential
Proposed

207
**Greenwich Peninsula
Riverside** (4)
Greenwich SE10
Aukett Swanke
Knight Dragon
20+ storeys
Residential
Proposed

208
**Greenwich Peninsula
Riverside** Plot M103
Greenwich SE10
CJCT Architects
Knight Dragon
23 storeys
Residential
Proposed

209
Greenwich Peninsula Riverside Plot M104
Greenwich SE10
Pilbrow and Partners
Knight Dragon
31 storeys
Residential
Approved

210
Greenwich Peninsula Riverside Plot M121
Greenwich SE10
Pilbrow and Partners
Knight Dragon
20 storeys
Residential
Approved

211
Love Lane Tower*
Greenwich SE18
HLM Architects
Love Street Woolwich
77m / 25 storeys
Residential
Proposed

212
Mast Quay (Phase 2 Block E)*
Greenwich SE18
Upchurch Associates
Comer Homes Group
67m / 22 storeys
Residential & Commercial
Proposed

213
Royal Arsenal Riverside Block A/ B*
Greenwich
-
Berkeley Homes PLC
20+ storeys
Residential
Status Unknown

214
Royal Arsenal Riverside Block C*
Greenwich SE18
PRP Architects
Berkeley Homes PLC
69m / 20 storeys
Residential
Approved

215
The Meridian Tower
Greenwich SE10
Patel Taylor
Peninsula Quays Ltd
118m / 32 storeys
Residential & Retail
Proposed

216
The Peninsula Tower
Greenwich
RTKL Associates
Arora International
23 storeys
Residential
Approved

217
Woolwich Town Centre Tower*
Greenwich SE18
Collado Collins
Tesco Stores Ltd / St James Investment
92m / 30 storeys
Residential & Retail
Approved

218
Broadway Chambers (Building 1)
Newham E15 4QS
Allies and Morrison
Telford Homes / Caraeno
123m / 39 storeys
Residential & Retail
Approved

219
Broadway Chambers (Building 2)
Newham
Allies and Morrison
Telford Homes/ Careano
20 storeys
Residential
Approved

220
Crown Wharf (Tower 1)
Newham E15
Allies and Morrison
Tower Properties
70m / 23 storeys
Residential
Approved

221
Crown Wharf (Tower 2)
Newham E15
Allies and Morrison
Tower Properties
70m / 24 storeys
Residential
Approved

222
Crown Wharf (Tower 3)
Newham E15
Allies and Morrison
Tower Properties
74m / 24 storeys
Residential
Proposed

223
First Avenue
Newham E15
Fletcher Priest Architecture Ltd
Westfield
92m / 22 storeys
Commercial & Retail
Approved

224
Glasshouse Gardens (Tower One)
Newham
Allies and Morrison
Lend Lease/ LCR
30 storeys
Residential
Proposed

225
206-214 High Street
Newham E15 2JA
MJP Architects
Alumno Developments
84 & 35 storeys
Residential & Commercial
Approved

226
Manhattan Loft Gardens
Newham E15
Skidmore Owing & Merrill
Manhattan Loft Corporation
149m / 43 storeys
Residential & Hotel
Approved

227
Stratford Plaza
Newham E15
Allies and Morrison / Stock Woolstencroft
Telford Homes
93m / 26 storeys
Residential & Commercial
Under construction

228
Stratford Tower
Newham E15
MJP
Alumno
26 storeys
Residential
Proposed

229
The Pump House*
Newham E16
Studio RHE
-
73m / 24 storeys
Residential & Retail
Under construction

230
2-12 Stratford High Street (Block A)
Newham E15
Jestico & Whiles
Telford Homes
117m / 35 storeys
Residential & Commercial
Approved

231
24 Tidal Basin Road
Newham E16
SOM
Hub Residential
76m / 25 storeys
Residential
Approved

232
Unite Stratford
Newham E15
BDP
UNITE Group
90m / 28 storeys
Residential & Retail
Under construction

234
Fresh Wharf (Block H)*
Barking and Dagenham IG11
Glenn Howells Architects / Jestico and Whiles
Countryside Properties / Fresh Wharf Developments
67m / 22 storeys
Residential
Approved

235
Trocoll House, Wakering Road*
Barking and Dagenham IG11
Dexter Moren Architects
Coplan Estates
67m / 22 storeys
Hotel & Retail
Approved

236
Vicarage Field*
Barking and Dagenham IG11
PRP Architects
LagMAR Holdings
70m / 23 storeys
Residential & Retail
Approved

CHAPTER 1

What determines the scale and location of tall buildings?

'London's face is its fortune, and it belongs to everyone'

Sir Neil Cossons OBE, Pro-Provost of the Royal College of Art and from 2000-07, Chairman of English Heritage

Since the Millennium, London has witnessed the construction of a series of tall buildings that have transformed the city's skyline – from the Gherkin, which gained planning permission in 2000, through to The Shard, which opened in 2012, to The Leadenhall Building and 20 Fenchurch Street which are completing this year. And there are many more to come in the next few years, a veritable tsunami of towers: 236 buildings are in the pipeline, 113 of which are already approved for planning.

Some observers fear that what is currently taking place in London is dangerously akin to a Dubai or Shanghai-style free for all, a pell-mell race to the sky, in which planners wave through applications and count the boroughs' development gains as a price well worth paying.

Against that, other planners and developers argue that the expansion of towers in London has taken place under the aegis of a sophisticated and highly developed planning regime, which broadly controls where tall buildings can be located and determines what they should, or rather what they should not, look like. Tall buildings such as One Canada Square, the Gherkin or The Shard, have enhanced London's status on the world stage, setting a visual marker for London as a powerful global player.

Tall buildings inevitably arouse controversy, all the more so in a city with such a rich historical fabric as London. The city's skyline belongs to everyone, and people's opinions often differ from those of the planning authorities, who themselves can clash over the many ambiguities that seem to riddle our planning regime. But the question that needs to be asked – and one which this study poses – is whether the planning process is working as best and as sensitively as it could.

Before that charge is properly examined, it is essential to clarify how the current system works. How do we go about making critical decisions on which tall buildings are allowed to be built and where? How do politicians, looking both to safeguard London's heritage but also to regenerate large swathes of the capital, play their part in influencing the process? And what exactly is driving this current surge in demand for tall buildings in the capital?

As a small but telling indication of the difficulties of the subject, the very term 'tall building' eludes an exact official definition. The Greater London Authority (GLA) defines tall buildings as 'those that are substantially taller than their surroundings' or 'cause a significant change to the skyline'. As a rule of thumb for its own purposes, the City of London says this translates to a height threshold of 75m above sea level.

London boroughs take their cue from the GLA, with local variations. The Lambeth Core Strategy, for example, defines tall buildings as developments over 25m high on sites adjacent to the Thames and buildings over 30m elsewhere.

This study has elected to consider tall buildings as structures with over 20 storeys plus those that vary significantly in scale from their surroundings.

1.1 Densification

London's population is growing twice as fast as the rest of the United Kingdom. From 2011 to 2012 alone, the capital's population grew by 1.3 per cent to 8.3 million. One in five of all UK births, around 120,000 per year, now takes place in London (ONS). Latest estimates indicate that London's population may exceed 10 million by 2031 and 11 million by 2050.

This rapidly accelerating growth is driven by a number of factors: high birth and immigration rates, increasing life expectancies, and a greater number of people choosing to stay in London for longer. It places enormous strains on life in the capital, most notably with regard to housing, which has become the most pressing priority for policy makers in London and the south east.

The Mayor of London's *2020 Vision*, published in 2013 to set out his ambitions for the capital, posits the need to create 400,000 new homes in the next decade, and one million by the mid-2030s. He also predicts that there will be an extra 450,000 jobs by 2023, making the availability of office space an issue only slightly less critical than housing.

Professor Tony Travers of the London School of Economics, writing for the Housing Forum, said: 'It cannot be a solution to the demand for housing in thriving places like London to move people ever further

City of London, 2025
© CPAT / Hayes Davidson / Jason Hawkes

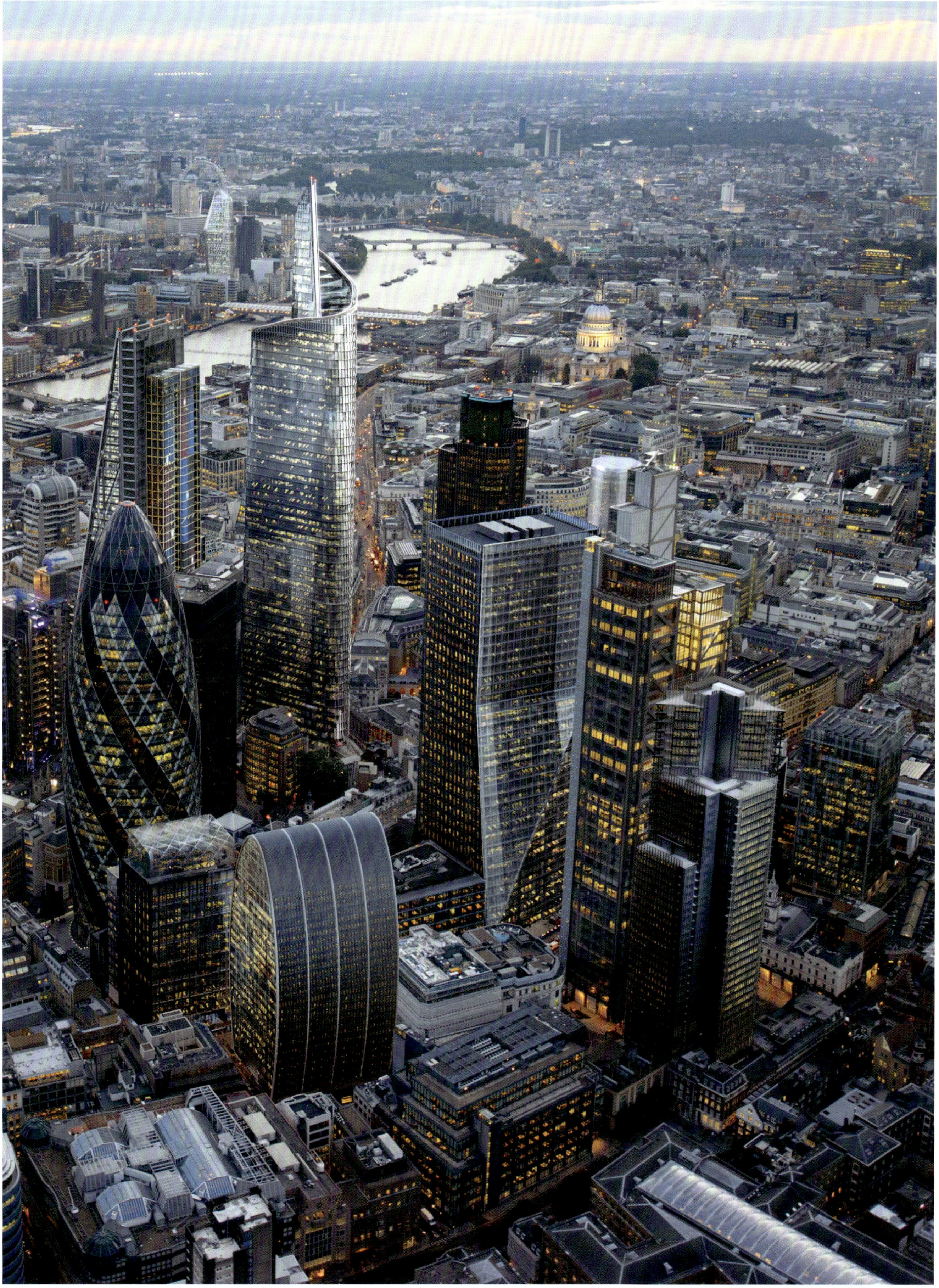

Below: GLA map of central London tall building clusters, with Central Activity Zone indicated in yellow

Bottom left: Projected population of London by 2050. Source: GLA Economics

Bottom right: Density rankings across global cities. Source: UN Population Estimates

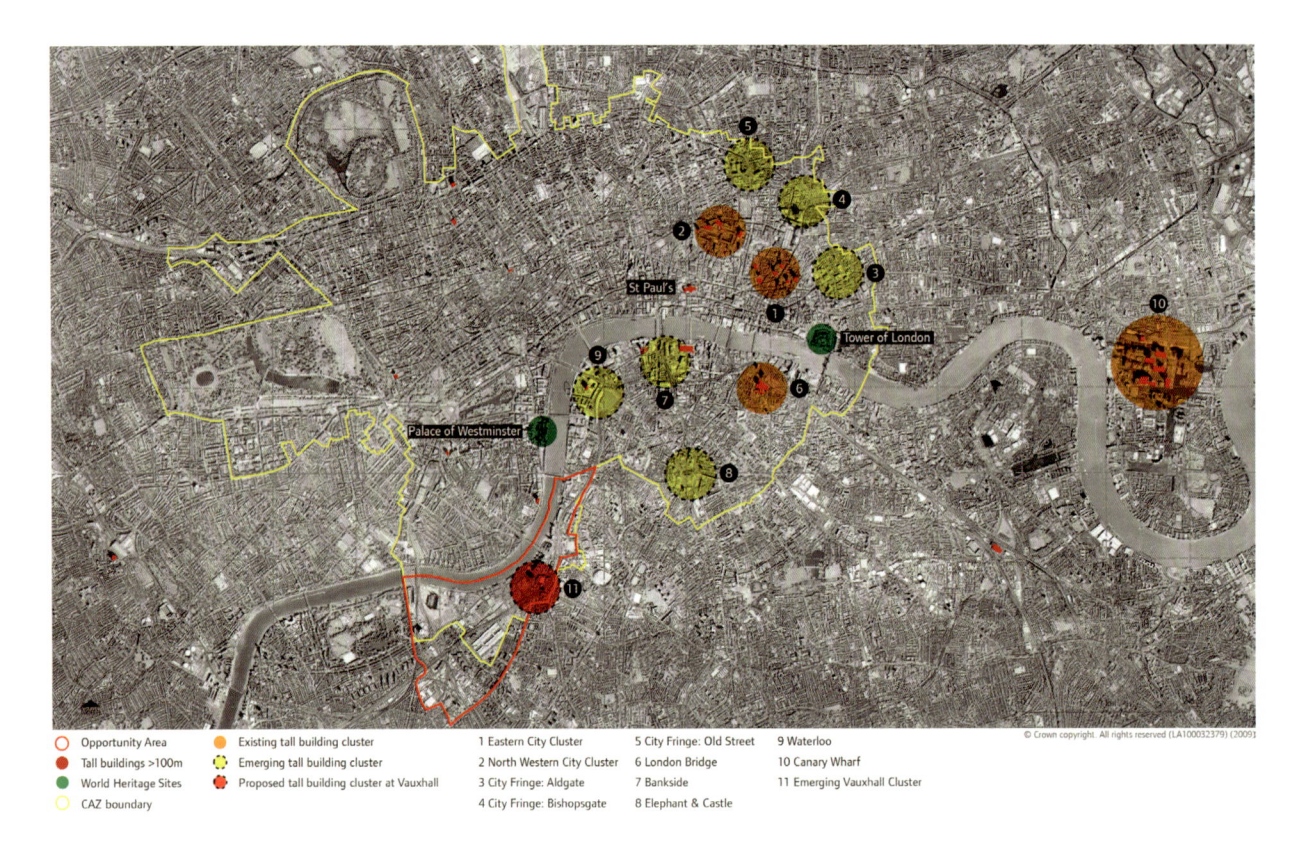

- ○ Opportunity Area
- ● Tall buildings >100m
- ● World Heritage Sites
- ○ CAZ boundary
- ● Existing tall building cluster
- ● Emerging tall building cluster
- ● Proposed tall building cluster at Vauxhall

1 Eastern City Cluster
2 North Western City Cluster
3 City Fringe: Aldgate
4 City Fringe: Bishopsgate
5 City Fringe: Old Street
6 London Bridge
7 Bankside
8 Elephant & Castle
9 Waterloo
10 Canary Wharf
11 Emerging Vauxhall Cluster

POPULATION GROWTH
Source: GLA Economics

Projected at 11.3 million by 2050 based on extension of London Plan scenario, driven by natural growth rate

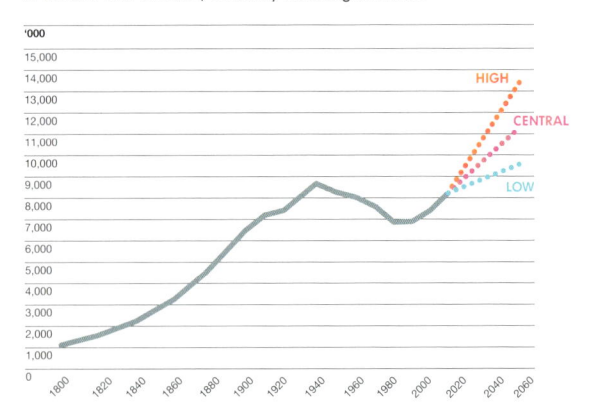

DENSITY RANKINGS ACROSS GLOBAL CITIES
Source: Using UN Population Estimates

City	Population	Area
Mumbai	17.3m	546km²
Hong Kong	17.2m	275km²
Singapore	5.3m	518km²
Istanbul	12.9m	1,347km²
Shanghai	21.8m	3,497km²
London	9.6m	1,623km²
Tokyo	37.2m	8,547km²
Madrid	6.1m	1,321km²
Paris	10.9m	2,845km²
Moscow	15.8m	4,403km²
Milan	5.2m	1,891km²
New York	20.7m	11,642km²

16 LONDON'S GROWING UP!

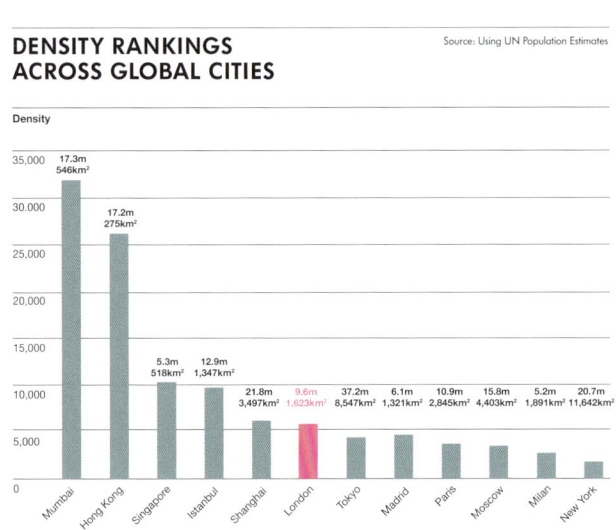

out in search of cheaper places to live. The critical issue is how to bring about significant increases in supply without resorting to building extensively in the green belt, or beyond.'

London's policy makers broadly agree with Professor Travers. Historically, high-density housing was associated with overcrowding, particularly in lower-income areas. Now, thanks to the close correlation between high urban density, low energy use for transport, and the desire to curb the spread of the city into the Green Belt, it is seen as a key solution for achieving a sustainable city, and is made explicit in the London Plan. In looking at the relative densities of other large city conurbations around the globe, London's existing density is in fact fairly low.

The formation of the Greater London Authority and the publication of the *Draft London Plan* in 2002 led to a new spatial strategy for London aimed at increasing densities and accessibility in order to create a more 'sustainable and compact city'. According to this strategy – which had been strongly urged in Richard Roger's 1999 Urban Task Force report – an increase in densities in highly accessible areas, can lead to positive economic growth, and more sustainable urban development, bringing many environmental and social advantages. Through combining mixed-use and mixed-tenure developments, particularly around public transport nodes, it argues that greater densities can bring more cohesive and sustainable communities, while halting urban sprawl. Following this approach, the London Plan sets targets for higher densities around London's public transport nodes.

The Commission for Architecture and the Built Environment (CABE), established in 1999 and merged into the Design Council in 2011, agreed with the strategy but also noted that: 'Higher density development leads to more intensive use of space and shared areas with implications for management, security and overall quality of life. Issues of noise, daylight, privacy and overlooking all become more acute as densities increase, requiring careful design.' Unless this is done, 'there is a risk of recreating the cramped and poor housing environments of the past.'

While tall residential buildings are one way of addressing London's acute housing demands, they are not necessarily the only option. Talking of the new homes required, the Mayor has said: 'These will not be high-rise rabbit hutches. They can be built with London's traditional materials – brick and stone and slate. We have introduced new room sizes of Parker Morris plus 10 per cent, and there are plenty of examples in London where high densities can be achieved without high-rise buildings.

'Where buildings are on top of or immediately adjacent to a transport hub, it may make sense to build high – depending on the historic or architectural context. There are some places such as Vauxhall or London Bridge where high-rise development is clearly right and has strong local support.

'London is not central Paris. We do not have a single architectural idiom, or a rule that no building should be more than 83 feet high. That gives us great flexibility. But it is simply not the case that good quality high-density housing must always involve tower blocks. Of the 400,000 homes we will need over the next ten years, the vast majority can be built on the brownfield Opportunity Areas we have identified.'

Many urban planners over the years have also argued that tall buildings are not the only way to achieve densification. In 2002, a Parliamentary Select Committee for Transport, Local Government and the Regions reported that, 'there is broad consensus amongst the witnesses that high rise is not the only or most efficient way to provide high densities. As the National Housing Federation pointed out, the Urban Task Force report, *Towards An Urban Renaissance*, found that that the same density could be provided by high, medium and low rise developments in different configurations.'

The Committee referred to the Georgian Group's submission on Lillington Garden Estate in Pimlico, which was designed by Darbourne and Darke in 1961-71, and showed that high density and low-rise could be compatible. Commented the Georgian Group: 'To some extent, Lillington Gardens was simply relearning the lessons of the Georgian era, where the typical urban terrace achieves a density of around 340 habitable rooms per hectare, compared with an average of around two-

Below: Ten ways to achieve the same density on a site

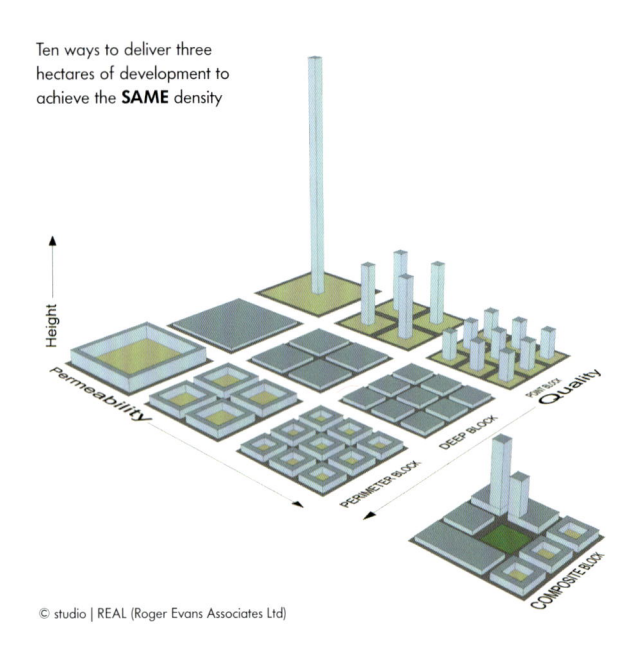

Ten ways to deliver three hectares of development to achieve the **SAME** density

© studio | REAL (Roger Evans Associates Ltd)

thirds that figure for a conventional post-war housing development.'

A report in 2013 from think tank Create Streets, entitled *Create Streets: Not just multi-storey estates*, was also highly critical of building tall residential blocks as a solution to London's housing crisis, arguing that building homes at street level can provide more homes than high-rise.

In fact the 2011 census shows the relatively low-rise London borough of Islington to have the highest population density of all local authorities across England and Wales, at 13,875 people per square km. Speaking at a recent NLA conference, Professor Tony Travers indicated that were the whole of Greater London to be developed at the same density, this could provide enough homes to increase London's population to 20 million, far and away enough to meet current demand.

London faces intense pressures to accommodate its expanding population, whether through more dense construction at low to mid-rise, building upwards or expanding out beyond the city's boundaries. Densification is at the heart of the London Plan and no change of policy is likely on this while London's population continues to grow.

1.2 The market

Commercial and residential land values in London are driven by a combination of factors – rising population, finite development land, a chronic shortage of housing, economic cycles and investor confidence, both domestically and internationally.

When land is at such a premium, particularly in central London, tall buildings with high plot ratios can be an effective way of making the best use of available space. They can also offer the most profit potential.

However, the large upfront investments make tall buildings vulnerable to economic downturns. *The Skyscraper Index*, formulated by the Barclays economist Andrew Lawrence in 1999, detects a strong correlation between the completion of tall buildings, which were started in boom times, and the arrival of financial crises. Certainly, London has its share of tall buildings that fell victim to the world economic crisis of 2008 onwards, most notably the Pinnacle in Bishopsgate which was to become the tallest building in the City of London but struggled with funding and is now being reengineered to meet current market conditions. The Shard was nearly derailed by the global downturn in late 2007.

However, with the onset of recovery recently, residential land values have risen – by over 20 per cent in the past year alone. Construction costs have also fallen – they currently sit 20 per cent below 2006 levels. And investor/developer confidence has returned, some of it money from China and other booming Far Eastern economies seeking a safe haven. Savills research has shown that 44 per cent of new residential developments have Asian owners, while the figure for the central London office market is 24 per cent.

In particular, demand for new tall buildings is being driven by the residential market. Some of this residential development is taking place in fast developing areas along the south bank of the Thames, while much is also happening in the Wood Wharf and South Quay area of Tower Hamlets. As AECOM explains in a paper

Above: Visualisation of the lobby at the Pinnacle © Hayes Davidson
Below: Aerial view of the proposed Pinnacle by KPF, City of London © Hayes Davidson
Below right: One Wood Wharf, by Herzog and de Meuron for Canary Wharf Group plc

published by the Council on Tall Buildings and Urban Habitat (CTBUH) in 2013: 'With office values, in real terms, no different to the levels they attained some 20 years or so ago, there are a number of office-led developments that are incorporating a residential element, sometimes in the same building, creating a new typology of mixed-use tower.'

The cost of tall buildings is one factor that drives many developers to aim for the luxury end of the market. A Knight Frank report, *Tall Towers 2012*, states that 'residential tower schemes are viable only when buyers are willing to pay a relatively high base price, starting at around £800-1,000 per sq ft. The higher the apartment, the higher the premium.'

And, of course, the more desirable the location, the greater the premium at any level. AECOM reports super prime residential schemes achieving between £2,500-£5,000 per sq ft.

The same height-price equation generally applies to commercial buildings too – the higher the floor, the more prestigious the address, and accordingly the steeper the rent.

Below: Opportunity Areas in the London Plan, courtesy of GLA

The potential returns for developers also depend on the costs of design and construction. Building a tower to the exceptional design quality required to win planning permission in itself makes the cost higher than most other forms of lower-level development.

AECOM estimates the construction costs of residential towers are about 10 per cent higher than commercial towers but that their respective values can differ markedly. The residential tower's value in a super-prime location can command premium sales/rental income.

1.3 Controls and policies

Planning in London is organised through a complex hierarchy of controls, from national level to regional level through to local authorities, which are required by law to draw up their own individual local plans. As well as stipulated planning parameters, there are also numerous specific guidances that relate to tall buildings. These include *Guidance on Tall Buildings* issued by English Heritage and CABE in 2007, as well as numerous heritage and protected view obligations, some of which derive from UNESCO's listing as World Heritage Sites the historical London landmarks of the Tower of London; the Royal Botanic Gardens at Kew; the Palace of Westminster and Westminster Abbey; and Maritime Greenwich.

Further complexity is introduced by the planning system's built-in flexibility, which allows for individual projects to depart from the policy norm if there is merit in doing so – many argue this also allows London to take a uniquely pragmatic approach.

1.4 The Mayor and the London Plan

The Mayor's London Plan, the overall strategic plan for London, outlines broad design guidelines for tall buildings in the capital, designates general areas where they should be located and the protected views they must not impede. These views are set out in detail in the London View Management Framework (see page 22).

In particular the London Plan specifies that tall buildings should generally be limited to sites in the Central Activity Zone (CAZ), Opportunity Areas, Areas of Intensification or town centres that have good access to public transport.

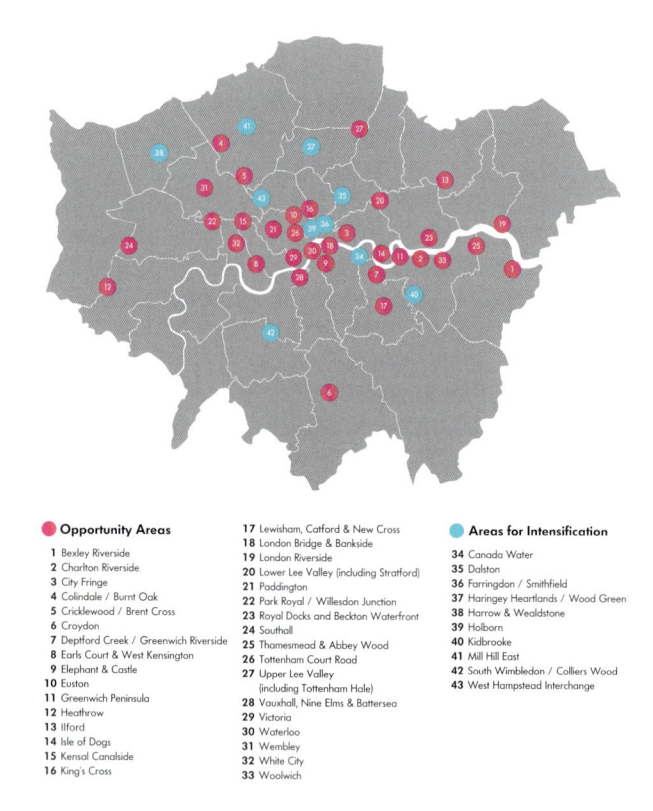

The London Plan specifies 33 Opportunity Areas (with an additional five proposed in the 2014 *Draft Further Alterations to the London Plan*) as the capital's major reservoir of brownfield land with significant capacity to accommodate new housing, commercial and other development, while the 10 Areas of Intensification (proposed to reduce to seven in 2014) are typically built-up areas with good existing or potential public transport accessibility which can support redevelopment at higher densities. Together, the opportunity areas have capacity for 490,300 additional jobs and 233,600 additional homes; while the intensification areas can accommodate 13,000 new jobs and a further 14,350 homes.

● **Opportunity Areas**
1 Bexley Riverside
2 Charlton Riverside
3 City Fringe
4 Colindale / Burnt Oak
5 Cricklewood / Brent Cross
6 Croydon
7 Deptford Creek / Greenwich Riverside
8 Earls Court & West Kensington
9 Elephant & Castle
10 Euston
11 Greenwich Peninsula
12 Heathrow
13 Ilford
14 Isle of Dogs
15 Kensal Canalside
16 King's Cross
17 Lewisham, Catford & New Cross
18 London Bridge & Bankside
19 London Riverside
20 Lower Lee Valley (including Stratford)
21 Paddington
22 Park Royal / Willesden Junction
23 Royal Docks and Beckton Waterfront
24 Southall
25 Thamesmead & Abbey Wood
26 Tottenham Court Road
27 Upper Lee Valley (including Tottenham Hale)
28 Vauxhall, Nine Elms & Battersea
29 Victoria
30 Waterloo
31 Wembley
32 White City
33 Woolwich

● **Areas for Intensification**
34 Canada Water
35 Dalston
36 Farringdon / Smithfield
37 Haringey Heartlands / Wood Green
38 Harrow & Wealdstone
39 Holborn
40 Kidbrooke
41 Mill Hill East
42 South Wimbledon / Colliers Wood
43 West Hampstead Interchange

The Mayor must be consulted on all planning applications that are of potential strategic importance to London, which naturally can include tall buildings. There is no specified height limit for tall buildings in London. However, there is a referral policy – buildings over 30m may be referred to the Mayor, or 25m if they are on the Thames. In the City of London, this rises to 150m. Where the Mayor and his officials are unhappy with the way the London Plan's injunctions have been interpreted by local borough planners – of whose powers, see following sections of this study – it is open to them to call in the tall tower proposal and subject it to further review.

A case in Southwark in December 2013, where the Mayor approved construction of 335 homes at Elephant and Castle, illustrates the use of this GLA power. Planning permission had been refused by Southwark Council for a 41-storey block on the site of Eileen House, Newington Causeway, close to Elephant and Castle. The Mayor chose to take over the application on the grounds that the area has overriding housing needs. After some alterations by the developer, the scheme was approved. The development sits within the Elephant and Castle Opportunity Area – one of the 33 areas designated by the Mayor with significant capacity for new development.

Policy 7.7 Location and design of tall and large buildings

Strategic
Tall and large buildings should be part of a plan-led approach to changing or developing an area by the identification of appropriate, sensitive and inappropriate locations. Tall and large buildings should not have an unacceptably harmful impact on their surroundings.

Planning decisions
Applications for tall or large buildings should include an urban design analysis that demonstrates the proposal is part of a strategy that will meet the criteria below. This is particularly important if the site is not identified as a location for tall or large buildings in the borough's LDF.

Tall and large buildings should:
a) generally be limited to sites in the Central Activity Zone, opportunity areas, areas of intensification or town centres that have good access to public transport
b) only be considered in areas whose character would not be affected adversely by the scale, mass or bulk of a tall or large building
c) relate well to the form, proportion, composition, scale and character of surrounding buildings, urban grain and public realm (including landscape features), particularly at street level
d) individually or as a group, improve the legibility of an area, by emphasising a point of civic or visual significance where appropriate, and enhance the skyline and image of London
e) incorporate the highest standards of architecture and materials, including sustainable design and construction practices
f) have ground floor activities that provide a positive relationship to the surrounding streets
g) contribute to improving the permeability of the site and wider area, where possible
h) incorporate publicly accessible areas on the upper floors, where appropriate
i) make a significant contribution to local regeneration.

Tall buildings:
a) should not affect their surroundings adversely in terms of microclimate, wind turbulence, overshadowing, noise, reflected glare, aviation, navigation and telecommunication interference
b) should not impact on local or strategic views adversely

The impact of tall buildings proposed in sensitive locations should be given particular consideration. Such areas might include conservation areas, listed buildings and their settings, registered historic parks and gardens, scheduled monuments, battlefields, the edge of the Green Belt or Metropolitan Open Land, World Heritage Sites or other areas designated by boroughs as being sensitive or inappropriate for tall buildings.

1.5 London View Management Framework

Key London views of St Paul's and the Palace of Westminster have been legally protected since 1976's Greater London Development Plan. The plan has been modified at various times subsequently, with the London View Management Framework (LVMF) being adopted in 2007 and revised in 2012. Today the framework seeks to 'designate, protect and manage' 27 views of London and some of its major landmarks.

'Designated views' include panoramas across substantial parts of London, views of landmarks framed by objects in the landscape, broad prospects along the River Thames or views of the urban townscape. Any new development proposed within one of these views is expected to demonstrate how it will make a positive contribution to the characteristics and composition of the view.

At the same time 13 viewing corridors, or 'protected vistas' as they are called, place additional consultation requirements on developments that exceed a certain height, within or adjacent to the sightline between the two places so as to preserve the ability to see the landmark as a focus of the view. It was because of the need to protect views of St Paul's that The Leadenhall Building (aka the Cheesegrater) has its distinctive tapered side.

Any new developments within these protected vistas which exceed a certain height threshold must be sent to the Mayor and affected local authority, who must consult English Heritage and, where the development affects the Tower of London, Historic Royal Palaces.

1.6 Secretary of State

The Secretary of State has the power to call-in planning applications for determination if they conflict with national policies, might have a 'significant long-term impact on economic growth', 'impact beyond their immediate boundaries', give rise to 'national controversy', or raise 'significant architectural and urban design issues'. So far, call-in powers have been used fairly rarely in London.

The decision of the Secretary of State on whether to grant planning permission following an appeal or the call-in of an application is informed by the report of an Inspector who nearly always holds a public inquiry into the proposal. Such decisions are 'quasi-judicial', and therefore particular care is needed in taking them. However, similar considerations also arise in the exercise of discretionary powers on planning matters, such as in deciding whether or not to call in a planning application or recover an appeal.

The Heron Tower, called in in 2001, and The Shard, called in in 2002, are two examples of buildings that went to public inquiry. The Heron Tower, in Bishopsgate, was opposed by English Heritage because of its proximity to St Paul's when viewed from Waterloo Bridge. CABE backed the design, but Deputy Prime Minister John Prescott ordered a public inquiry, which found in the developer's favour. The tower's height was subsequently increased from 183m to its current 230m without objection.

---

13 views are protected by the London View Management Framework:

- Alexandra Palace to St Paul's Cathedral
- the summit of Parliament Hill to St Paul's Cathedral
- the summit of Parliament Hill to the Palace of Westminster
- Parliament Hill, at the prominent oak tree east of the summit, to Palace of Westminster
- the viewing gazebo at Kenwood House to St Paul's Cathedral
- the summit of Primrose Hill to St Paul's Cathedral
- the summit of Primrose Hill to the Palace of Westminster
- Greenwich Park, north east of the General Wolfe statue, to St Paul's Cathedral
- Blackheath Point, near the orientation board, to St Paul's Cathedral
- Westminster Pier to St Paul's Cathedral
- King Henry VIII's Mound in Richmond Park to St Paul's Cathedral
- the centre of the bridge over the Serpentine to the Palace of Westminster
- The Queen's Walk at City Hall to The White Tower at the Tower of London

Below: Strategic viewpoints protected by the LVMF, courtesy of GLA
Bottom: Components of a designated view, courtesy of GLA

Below (top to bottom): View from Alexandra Palace – south western section (zoomed in) courtesy of GLA; Telephoto view from Blackheath to St Paul's, courtesy of GLA; View from Greenwich Park (zoomed in) courtesy of GLA; View from Kenwood, courtesy of GLA; View from Parliament Hill to Palace of Westminster (zoomed in) courtesy of GLA

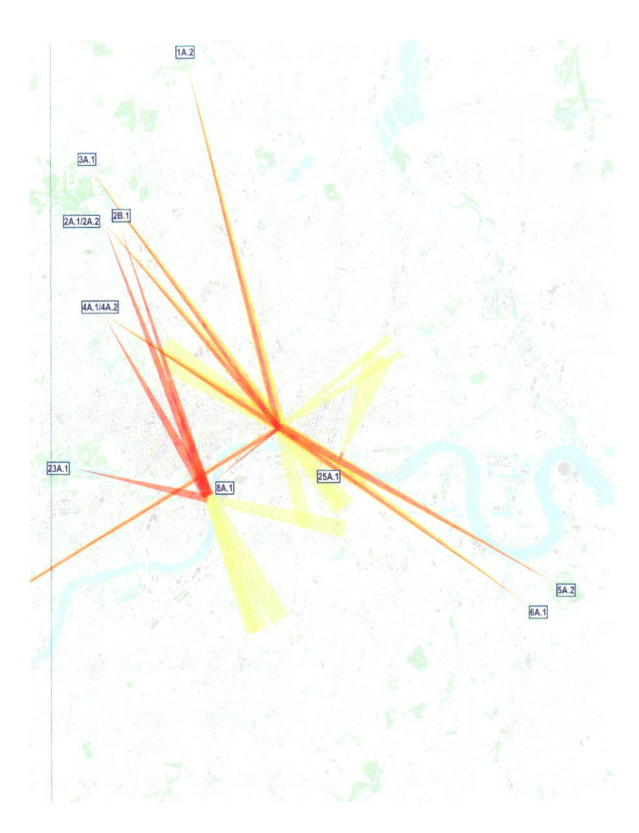

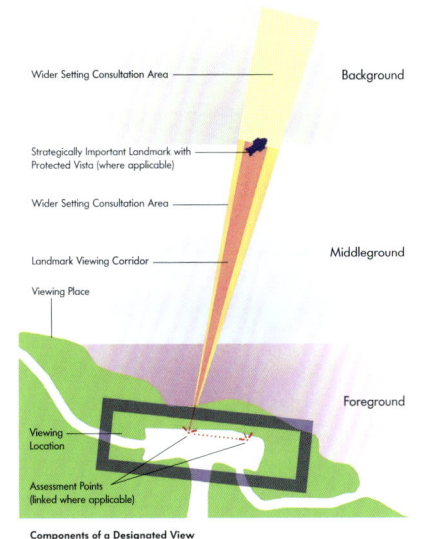

Below: The Barbican complex.
Photography: Agnese Sanvito

The Shard's public inquiry the following year arose out of objections from CABE and English Heritage as well as the Royal Parks Foundation. Again, the public inquiry found for the developer and his architects Renzo Piano.

The most recent example of the Government calling in a tall building proposal is the redevelopment around the Shell Centre in Waterloo, where a decision is expected in early 2014.

The Civil Aviation Authority (CAA) also has a say in height issues, stating that London buildings over 1,000 feet infringe airspace. If planners grant permission for anything in excess of 1,000 feet, the CAA can request the Secretary of State to call in and determine the application. It was because the CAA expressed concerns about The Shard's positioning in relation to the Heathrow approach that its proposed height was reduced from 400m to 300m. London City Airport also influences the height of buildings in its vicinity and flight paths.

1.7 Boroughs and Local Plans

The 32 London boroughs, together with the City of London Corporation, are responsible for preparing Local Plans for their own areas, which determine what can be built where, but must ensure they conform broadly to the Mayor's London Plan.

The London Plan states that: 'The Mayor will work with boroughs to identify locations where tall and large buildings might be appropriate, sensitive or inappropriate. He will help them develop local strategies to help ensure these buildings are delivered in ways that maximise their benefits and minimise negative impacts locally and across borough boundaries as appropriate.' (Policy 7.28)

1.8 The City of London

Concentrated in the City's square mile is London's densest cluster of tall buildings. Office towers, and the residential complex of the multi-purpose Barbican Centre, have been constructed here since the 1960s. When London's financial centre of gravity threatened to move towards Canary Wharf in the late 1990s, the City of London authorities responded by loosening its restrictive planning regime and encouraged a new tranche of tall building development, starting with the architecturally adventurous 'Gherkin', which led the way in establishing new design aspirations. Many of the world's elite architects have added to the City's transformation, often with dedicated public access areas at the very top of their buildings, such as at the Gherkin and 20 Fenchurch Street (the 'Walkie Talkie' tower) – something encouraged by the City's planning department as a vital component of their approval.

Bottom: The City of London, with The Heron Tower in the foreground and St Paul's to the far right

Below: City of London Core Strategy 2011, showing areas inappropriate for tall buildings

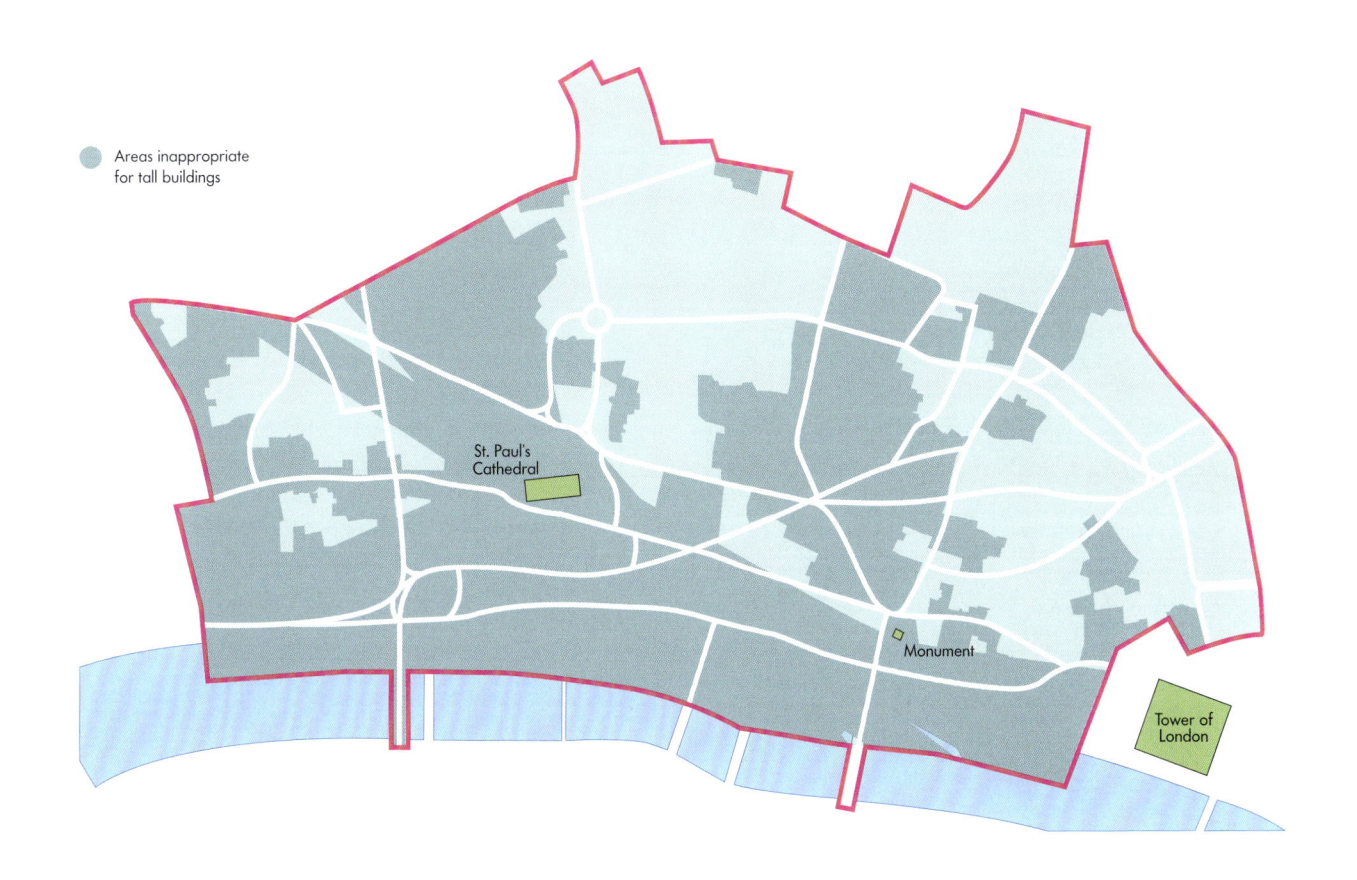

Areas inappropriate for tall buildings

St. Paul's Cathedral

Monument

Tower of London

Below: Eastern Cluster of the City of London, viewed from the South Bank, courtesy of GLA

Below: Proposed redevelopment of King's Reach Tower, by KPF for King's Reach Estates Ltd / CIT Real Estate LLP

1.9 Southwark

Southwark, sitting across the Thames from the City, has become home to some of London's tallest buildings including The Shard and the old King's Reach Tower as well as number of current consents for new tall buildings. The local authority drew up a borough-wide *Strategic Tall Building Research Paper* in 2010.

It defines tall buildings as those higher than 30m (or 25m in the Thames Policy Area) – approximately the height of a 7-10 storey office block. In low-scale areas, anything significantly higher is regarded as a tall building even if below 30m.

The Strategy designates areas appropriate for tall buildings, which broadly reflect key 'Opportunity Areas' in the borough: Bankside, Borough and London Bridge;

Like the London boroughs, the City of London, which is a unitary authority, has a Core Strategy which sets a framework for how the City should develop. In it, it defines tall buildings not by a specific figure but as those which 'significantly exceed the height of their surroundings.' The GLA stipulates that the City must refer to it any building with a proposed height of 150m or over.

A key concern for the City of London is the preservation of strategic views of St Paul's Cathedral, which are protected by a policy known as 'St Paul's Heights' that limits the height of buildings within these sightlines. The policy has been in operation since 1938.

These protected views have a significant impact on where tall buildings can be located in the City. The area referred to as 'the eastern cluster', broadly between Leadenhall Market, Liverpool Street Station and Fenchurch Street Station, is where the City supports the development of more tall buildings, while the west of the City and its riverside have been kept free of tall buildings. On the eastern fringe of the City, Aldgate is another area with significant development potential and the City specifies that tall buildings may be appropriate on certain sites.

Below: View produced by Southwark Council to determine height of buildings along Blackfriars Road, courtesy of Southwark Council

Below: Proposal for Elizabeth House, by David Chipperfield Architects for Chelsfield and London & Regional Properties

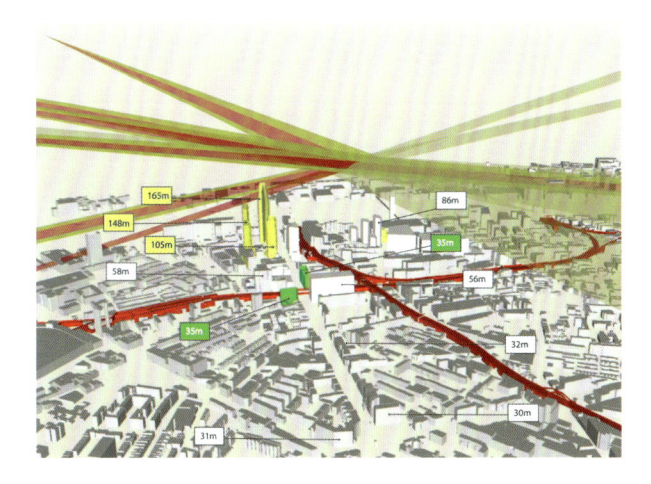

Elephant and Castle; Peckham and Nunhead; Aylsebury; and Canada Water.

To illustrate the level of detail boroughs go into, Southwark's 2010 tall building study of the Bankside, Borough and London Bridge area and a second study of the Elephant and Castle area are illuminating.

The first of these studies was undertaken in two stages. Having identified general areas where tall buildings could be located, a more detailed study provided a comprehensive analysis of the areas to identify specific sites where tall buildings would be appropriate and the particular design opportunities, constraints and sensitivities for tall buildings on these sites. Southwark used a three dimensional model to undertake a desk-based view analysis of strategic, local and dynamic views in order to understand the potential effect that tall building development in these views.

The same micro-analysis was carried out in the *Elephant and Castle Supplementary Planning Guidance*, which was approved by the council in February 2004. The SPG recognised the important role that regeneration of the Elephant and Castle would play in the wider development of London South Central as a focus for investment and jobs.

1.10 City of Westminster

The City of Westminster has taken a very different approach. With over 11,000 listed buildings, a World Heritage Site, Royal Parks and 51 Conservation Areas (which cover 85 per cent of the district), its rich urban fabric has led to a low-to-mid rise buildings regime, generally no higher than six to eight storeys, with some notable exceptions such as Big Ben, the Hilton Hotel, Kensington Barracks and New Zealand House. As a Buro Happold study in 2000 put it, 'the likely detrimental impact on [the area's historical buildings] is the reason why the approach to high buildings in Westminster has always been one of resistance.'

However, the council has designated locations where tall buildings may be permitted – Tottenham Court Road, Victoria and Paddington. There are several tall buildings in Paddington and Victoria – none of which is as tall as the developers originally envisaged.

Surrounded by a number of local authorities with a more favourable approach to tall building development, Westminster has also been quite vocal in its opposition to tall buildings that sit outside of its own boundaries. In response to Lambeth Council's permission for the Elizabeth House scheme in Waterloo, Westminster Council deputy leader Robert Davis wrote to Lambeth Council's cabinet member for housing and regeneration, Pete Robbins, saying: 'Westminster and English Heritage do not agree that your decisions have paid sufficient regard to the national policy on protection of the historic environment and the World Heritage Site, as required by the National Planning Policy Framework.

'The skyline of London is changing dramatically, and in places not for the better. The GLA and boroughs such as yours are repeating the mistakes of the 1960s, but now on a much greater scale, allowing development which will scar the character of London irreparably. I think it highly likely that future generations will look back on this period and regard it as one where rationality and sensitivity by decision makers were completely missing.'

After the Government rejected its call to call in the application, Westminster obtained from the High Court last November a Judicial Review of the Government's decision to wave it through. The result is due before the summer.

Resolving cross-boundary disputes over tall buildings is something of a grey area. Under the National Policy Planning Framework, councils are only bound to consult with the neighbouring local authority through a 'duty to co-operate'. Ultimately in disputes, the final decision rests with the democratically elected Mayor, subject to legal review.

1.11 S106 and CIL

Many tall building planning permissions come with financial obligations under Section 106 of the Town and Country Planning Act 1990 (as amended), which are commonly known as S106 agreements. The aim is to mitigate or offset the impact any development has on the area, in terms of existing amenities and infrastructure. The commonest uses of planning obligations are to secure affordable housing, new schools, health clinics, new spaces and the infrastructure necessary to support the new building, which the borough might not otherwise be able to afford.

The correct use of S106 agreements is sometimes not clear. In March 2010 the Government consulted London boroughs and were told more clarity of guidance is required on whether a planning application can be refused if S106 obligations are refused. The system is now in transition to the Community Infrastructure Levy (CIL), which has a more clear-cut approach relating the size of the developer's contribution directly to the development's square footage.

From the local authority's point of view, tall building proposals can offer the opportunity to exact considerable community benefits as a quid pro quo from the developer.

Sellar, the developers behind The Shard, for example, contributed £37 million in S106 to Southwark Council. This payment was allocated to:

– £25 million on a new train station concourse, new plaza, refurbishment of London Bridge Street, and a new 30 per cent bigger bus station, re-orientated to create a new public transport interchange;
– £2.2 million refurbishment of St Thomas Street, pedestrianisation of Great Maze Pond and Joiner Street;
– £5 million employment programme – 40 per cent of the staff at The View from The Shard are Southwark residents, while there is a now a dedicated employment and training team to maximise employment opportunities and provide training for local residents;
– £1 million public art programme;
– £4 million payment to Guy's Hospital to create a new modern access to the campus.

1.12 English Heritage

English Heritage, which is the Government's statutory adviser on historical assets, is one of the most active participants in the tall buildings debate in London. It has made a number of interventions that have led to public inquiries, including that for The Shard. Its opposition to the Heron Tower in 2001 led to an inquiry, where it was described by Mayor Ken Livingstone as 'an obscure monastic order', while former City Planning Officer Peter Rees once described English Heritage as the 'Heritage Taliban'.

In 2007, English Heritage and CABE jointly produced *Guidance on tall buildings* to help evaluate tall building proposals (first published in 2003). It is still regarded as best practice nationally with regard to tall building assessments. Though not constituting national policy, it sets out criteria for evaluating tall building proposals and is considered a useful reference in any evidence base.

Below: London Bridge Quarter piazza © Sellar Property Group

The guidance is positive about tall buildings' contribution to city life, but it cautions that they can also be harmful. 'In many cases where they have been unpopular, one of their principal failings is that many were designed with a lack of appreciation of the context in which they were to sit.'

The guidance strongly recommends that local authorities should identify appropriate locations for tall buildings in their development plan documents, saying: 'Such an approach will ensure that tall buildings are properly planned as part of an exercise in place-making informed by a clear long-term vision, rather than in an ad hoc, reactive, piecemeal manner.'

In addition to considering the wider objectives of sustainable urban design that apply to all new development, the guidance says local authorities should ensure that tall buildings take into account the historic context of the wider area. The authorities should carry out a character appraisal of the immediate context, identifying those elements that create local character and other important features and constraints, including: natural topography; urban grain; significant views of skylines; scale and height; streetscape; landmark buildings and areas and their settings, including backdrops, and important local views, prospects and panoramas. They should also identify opportunities where tall buildings might enhance the overall townscape and identify sites where the removal of past 'mistakes' might achieve a similar outcome.

Paragraph 4.4 of the guidance states: 'To be acceptable, any new tall building should be in an appropriate location, should be of first class design quality in its own right and should enhance the qualities of its immediate location and wider setting. It should produce more benefits than costs to the lives of those affected by it. Failure on any of these grounds will make a proposal unacceptable to CABE and English Heritage.'

Many other detailed recommendations are included in the guidance, including the importance of the base of tall building's effect on streetscape, and sustainability to exceed the latest regulations for energy use/carbon emissions.

Today, officials at English Heritage are keen to clarify that they are not opposed to tall buildings in London *per se* but many feel the evaluation process for assessing them is flawed. Said Nigel Barker, Planning and Conservation Director for London at EH at an NLA think tank on the subject: 'One of our frustrations is that the value of existing identity and character of areas does not seem to play as much role as it should do when being balanced against what are seen to be economic and other environmental benefits which are produced by tall buildings… There does not seem to be quite so much of a level playing field.'

1.13 UNESCO

The United Nations Educational, Scientific and Cultural Organisation (UNESCO) also plays an influential role in London's tall building story. Tall building planning applications within World Heritage Sites or their settings require the authorities to carefully consider the impact on the Outstanding Universal Value, authenticity and integrity of the World Heritage Site.

World Heritage Sites are places of Outstanding Universal Value, as set out in the 1972 UNESCO Convention Concerning the Protection of the World Cultural and Natural Heritage (the World Heritage Convention). As a State Party to the Convention, the United Kingdom is required to protect, conserve, present and transmit to future generations its World Heritage Sites.

London has four World Heritage Sites: Maritime Greenwich; the Tower of London; Palace of Westminster and Westminster Abbey, including St Margaret's Church; and Royal Botanic Gardens at Kew.

In all cases likely to have a significant impact on the value, authenticity and integrity of a World Heritage Site, pre-application consultation and discussions must be carried out with the planning authority and regional English Heritage staff to ensure that all the implications are fully understood and explicitly portrayed in supporting illustrative material.

The UNESCO World Heritage Committee has asked to be informed by national governments of proposals for major restorations or interventions which may affect the Outstanding Universal Value of a World Heritage Site.

They ask for notice to be given as soon as possible in order to help ensure the Outstanding Universal Value of the property is fully preserved. As English Heritage points out, this process raises problems in terms of defining whether developments will have an adverse impact on Outstanding Universal Value and of timing since the World Heritage Committee meets only once a year while in the UK planning decisions are normally taken more rapidly. In some cases, it may be appropriate to refer cases before submission of an actual planning application.

The decision on whether or not to refer cases to UNESCO is taken by the Department for Culture, Media and Sport (DCMS). They will first seek the advice of English Heritage and ask for English Heritage staff in the relevant regional office to be consulted at an early stage by planning authorities on all cases with significant potential impact on Outstanding Universal Value. All cases for which English Heritage requests call-in because of impact on Outstanding Universal Value will be considered for potential referral to the UNESCO World Heritage Committee. English Heritage will also advise DCMS on whether cases should be referred at an earlier stage of their development.

Below: The Tower of London, with The City from South Bank

UNESCO's intervention in a planning application is very rare but is always controversial when it does occur. In September 2012, for example, it threatened to delay a string of high-profile schemes near London's Waterloo Station because, it claimed they would damage from the Palace of Westminster, a World Heritage Site.
It has also flagged up concerns about a number of other schemes along the South Bank, including redevelopment around the Shell Centre at Waterloo.

Some critics argue that UNESCO has too much influence on development in London. While UNESCO has no direct power over planning decisions, it can ultimately remove World Heritage status from sites if they are significantly altered by new building developments.

World Heritage Site status is a highly prized listing, and observers fear that its removal would both damage London's cultural reputation and the significant tourism economy it brings.

Deputy mayor for planning Sir Edward Lister says the GLA will fight for growth. 'We understand their concerns but have to balance them with the demands of an expanding city,' he said. 'It's all about moderation from both sides.'

1.14 Right to Light

A neighbour's 'right to light', which is protected under planning law, can also play a significant role in influencing the development and height of towers. Redevelopment

Below: 20 Fenchurch Street, by Rafael Viñoly Architects for Land Securities and Canary Wharf Group plc

within the Square Mile often involves infringements of rights of light due to the dense built form and the need to make efficient use of scarce land resources. Any development which interferes with a legal right of light entitles the owner of that right to seek an injunction preventing development and/or compensation for the loss of light.

In an important ruling in 2011, known as the *Heaney* case, the Court granted a mandatory injunction requiring the developer of a redeveloped office block in Leeds to remove two floors because they blocked the light of a property next door. The decision came as a surprise to many as not only had the building work finished but one of the floors had already been let to a tenant. As a consequence of *Heaney*, neighbours who would previously have agreed to release rights of light (subject to adequate compensation) could now re-consider seeking an injunction, often dramatically affecting the viability and funding of schemes.

As part of the original planning application for the Walkie Talkie tower, the owners of the site at 20 Fenchurch Street had successfully negotiated with a number of individuals that were considered likely to suffer sufficient infringement of their rights to light. As a result of *Heaney*, however, the rights of lights of these neighbours had to be re-assessed. Seven instances were identified by the Court where the loss of light was considered to be of an extent that an injunction could be granted to prevent the development, with the remaining properties suitable for compensation.

The Corporation of London decided to use its planning powers to provide immunity from these claims to rights of light, by invoking Section 237 which is designed to protect developments which will provide economic benefits to the surrounding area. By doing so, the Walkie Talkie tower was provided with immunity from any rights of lights claims that could limit or prevent its development.

While 'rights to light' are rightly designed to protect those who would suffer from the loss of light as the result of a new development, in some cases uncertainty around its application in terms of timing and the scale of compensation has had the effect of holding developers to 'ransom' and thus towers could be reduced in height to avoid the delay and significant costs it poses to a scheme.

1.15 The Crown

The Prince of Wales has long taken a close interest in British architecture, presenting himself as an Everyman speaking for the people of this country – even at the risk of abusing his position through what critics have called 'unconstitutional, behind-the-scenes meddling' in the democratic process. One of his most striking interventions occurred in 2001 when he rallied strongly against tall buildings in London, saying: 'The City of London is, without doubt, a hugely successful financial centre – but it is a social disaster,' at a conference, *Building for the 21st Century*.

The Prince argued that tall buildings can wreck the 'sensitive balance' of London's urban environment. 'They will, by their very geometry and scale, always struggle to relate to the spaces a city needs in order to work successfully. They cast long shadows; they darken streets and suck life from them; they tend to violate the sense of public space so vital to a living street, either by requiring a plaza to give them light, or by refusing to align with existing buildings because of the difficulties of entering and servicing them without a large and cluttered forecourt.

'They also create "hot spots" of pedestrian movement that are a major burden on nearby stations and pavements, and because their forms of architectural expression are towering pieces of sculpture, rather than a well mannered contribution to the public realm, they seldom blend into the either the streetscape or the skyline with good aesthetic manners.'

The Prince, nevertheless, stated he was not opposed to tall buildings but that they must 'fit in'. He said: 'If new towers are to be built, they should stand together to establish a new skyline, and not compete with or confuse what is currently there – as has already happened to a depressing and disastrous extent... If clustered, then the virtue of height becomes something that can, in the hands of creative architects, be truly celebrated.'

As well as arguing for a cluster approach, the Prince called for tall buildings to be designed as mixed-use for a variety of homes and business. And he urged more attention be paid to the base and apex of structures. 'At the base, new buildings should properly address the streetscape and help define a public realm that is truly public in form and function.'

Tall building's sustainability credentials also drew the Prince's ire. 'Towers, because of their very structural demands, rely on huge amounts of electricity to power their lifts, air conditioning and other infrastructure. You cannot usually open windows – so nature's cooling system is shut down. Heat losses escalate as one builds higher.

'One of the fundamental principles of sustainable development is the idea of building for change; the construction of buildings that can 'learn' and adapt to new and unforeseen circumstances over time. This is extremely difficult to achieve with very tall buildings.'

The Prince's views evidently stirred debate amongst the profession but it is unclear as to how influential they proved. Certainly, no recent tall building proposal appears to have been derailed by the Prince's intervention in the way that his attack on Lord Roger's Chelsea Barracks scheme for the Qataris was perceived. But his views are reflected by a number of other urban thinkers and many in the public at large.

Right: The developing London skyline, looking west
© Hayes Davidson

1.16 Residents and Neighbourhood Plans

Some years ago the Government noted that resistance from local communities to proposals for new buildings, including towers, and economic development within their neighbourhoods is often a consequence of their lack of opportunity to influence the nature of that development. Communities, the Government said, can feel unable to ensure that development meets local needs and takes satisfactory account of the tensions between development and conservation, environmental quality and pressure on services. These concerns often manifested in objections to planning applications or may be reflected in the policy of the local planning authority. And the current system, it said, can sometimes lead to development taking place against the wishes of the community, being delayed by objections (which could be at expense to both business and the local planning authority) or blocked altogether.

It was to overcome these problems of top-down planning that the Localism Act was introduced in 2011, giving new rights to communities to shape local development through involvement in drawing up Neighbourhood Plans.

However, one of the Government's principal objectives in neighbourhood planning is that it increases the rate of growth. Therefore, neighbourhood planning cannot lead to a lower rate of growth than is established in the local development plan. If a Neighbourhood Plan attempts to slow the local rate of economic development, it will be revoked by the Government.

How this new localism plays out with regard to unpopular new tall building proposals has yet to be established. It is certainly the case that local boroughs go to enormous efforts to consult locally about their development plans; as do developers looking to win approval for a new tall building. But it is equally the case that local opposition to a new tall building does not necessarily prevent the development. And many residents across London have accused their councils of favouring development of tall towers against the wishes of the local community.

From a developer's point of view, Neighbourhood Plans should allow for greater certainty of the success of any proposal. Indeed, developers will be able to approach neighbourhood communities with an offer of financial support to promote a Neighbourhood Plan which explicitly identifies a specific development proposal of the kind that the developer would wish to take forward.

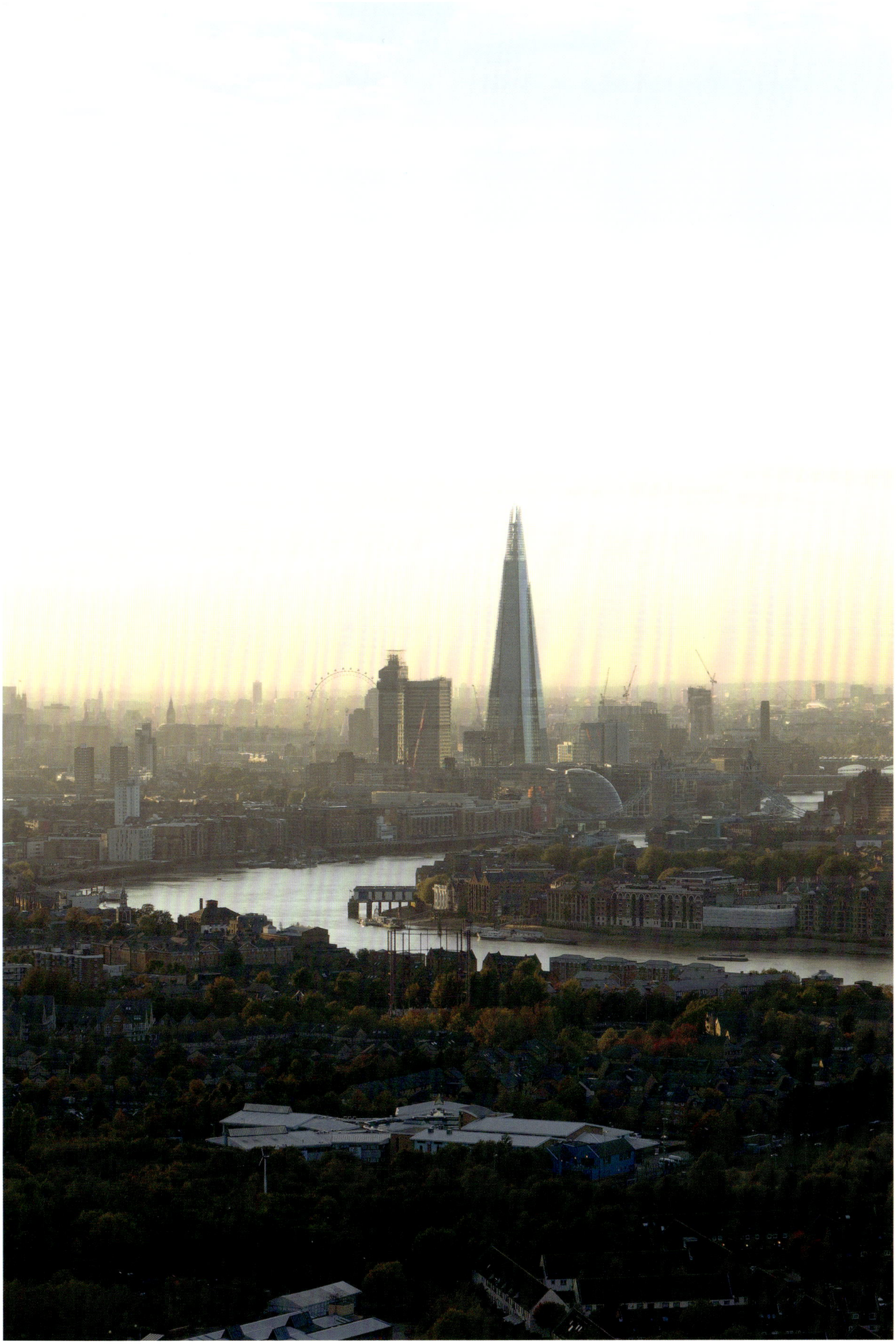

CHAPTER 2

Half a century of tall building in London

Below: Senate House and Library, designed by Adams Holden & Pearson. Photography: Studio Jaanus Limited, 1936. Courtesy of RIBA Library Photographs Collection

Bottom: Great Arthur House, within the Golden Lane Estate, designed by Chamberlin Powell & Bon. Photography: Reginald Hugo de Burgh Galwey, 1957. Courtesy of RIBA Library Photographs Collection

2.1 Pre 1960s

London's first tall buildings – St Paul's and other churches aside – were built in the 1920s and 1930s, several decades after Chicago's and New York's steel-frame structures had started reaching higher for the sky than had ever before been possible. The earliest buildings were hardly skyscrapers – Adelaide House, built in the City between 1921-25, was an 11-storey office block, 45m high. The London Transport headquarters, at 55 Broadway, trumped it in 1929 by just 8m and, in 1937, Senate House in Russell Square by nearly 20m.

In 1930, the London Building Act raised the maximum height of buildings from 80ft to 100ft. At that time, the length of the Fire Brigade's ladders was the main influence on restricting building heights. The City of London Corporation also introduced its own height restrictions in 1938 to protect views of St Paul's, which tied building heights to street widths.

In 1951 the London County Council (LCC) – now in control of London's planning – unveiled its County of London Development Plan, which set varying plot ratios to limit the amount of floor space that should be built on a site. However, the Plan did not control height, allowing tall buildings to be considered on their merits.

The first wave of truly tall London buildings came after the Second World War when residential buildings were created as part of the country's economic and social reconstruction. The London County Council, inspired by Le Corbusier's utopian vision of decent homes for all and steering by the 1944 Abercrombie Plan, wished to rebuild large swathes of London, clearing what was left of the slums after the ravages of war-time bombing. The counterpart of moving many of London's inhabitants out to new towns was the high-rise residential tower, built for mainly working class inhabitants. When the Conservative government in 1956 chose to pump-prime the new housing market by offering higher public subsidies the higher the building, the tall buildings boom took off.

Designed along Modern Movement and Brutalist lines, in rough concrete and often with walkways high above the ground, they rose to 50m and above on housing estates all over east and south London, and were initially considered to be quite successful. Only in the early 1970s were they perceived as bleak and inhuman, by which point more than 300 had been built by the LCC and the Greater London Council (GLC, which replaced the LCC in 1965).

The first high-rise tower block was Great Arthur House, part of the Golden Lane estate in Cripplegate. When completed in 1957 it was the first London residential tower block over 50m, and the first in the City of London.

Below: Balfron Tower, Poplar, designed by Ernö Goldfinger, Image: 1965. Courtesy of RIBA Library Photographs Collection
Bottom: Trellick Tower, North Kensington, designed by Ernö Goldfinger. Image: 1972. Courtesy of RIBA Library Photographs Collection

Bottom right: Cromwell Tower in The Barbican, designed by Chamberlin Powell & Bon. Photography: John Maltby, 1973. Courtesy of RIBA Library Photographs Collection

Right: Ronan Point, West Ham (after building collapse), designed by Newham Department of Planning and Architecture. Image: 1968. Courtesy of RIBA Library Photographs Collection
Below: Ronan Point and neighbouring tower blocks (built 1966-1972). Image: 1986. Courtesy of RIBA Library Photographs Collection

38 LONDON'S GROWING UP!

Below: Model of the Barbican development for the 'New Sights of London' exhibition, 1960. Courtesy of the London Metropolitan Archives

2.2 Residential towers in the 1960s and 1970s

The 1960s was the age of the residential tower block. Like stalagmites, they rose all over London's slums and war-blitzed neighbourhoods as local authorities strove to provide thousands of new homes.

The speed of their construction was driven by the adoption of 'large panel system building', mainly the Swedish Larsen-Nielsen system, which was licensed to Taylor Woodrow-Anglian. These fast-track systems used factory-made pre-cast concrete floors and wall panels as well as industrially produced kitchens which were assembled on site. Wates developed its own system in conjunction with Ove Arup.

The first structure erected in the UK of this type was for the LCC in 1963, and in 1965 Newham Council commissioned nine, twenty-two storey Larsen-Nielsen blocks. Pleasing architectural features were not part of the package; the name of the game was speed and cheapness.

By contrast, Balfron Tower (1968) and the Trellick Tower (1972) were two more distinctive residential towers designed by Ernö Goldfinger, the Hungarian-born, Le Corbusier-inspired architect who was a leading figure in British architecture throughout the 1950s and 1960s. Balfron Tower, in Poplar, stood 27 storeys and 276ft high and was constructed using in-situ concrete. With its 146 homes, and characteristic separate lift and service tower, it was the tallest housing block in Europe at the time and was Grade II listed in 1996.

Trellick Tower in North Kensington was built between 1968 and 1972, with 31 storeys and standing at 98m. Its 217 flats were organised into eight different apartment types, with windows on both sides. Although Goldfinger himself was an occupant, basing his office there, the tower quickly became seen as over-large, inhuman and possessing no community spirit, and it was blighted by crime and estate management failures. It was often described as a vertical slum. However, over time, with the introduction of 'right to buy' council homes, many of the apartments were bought up by tenants, and in the 1980s a new residents' association drove a number of improvements to its security and management. It has gradually become quite a fashionable address and in 1998 was Grade II* listed in recognition of its iconic status and architectural significance.

If Trellick Tower stood at the time for the dark side of tall residential buildings and social engineering, Ronan Point sounded the death knell – at least, for the next 40 odd years. The 22-storey tower in Canning Town, built in 1966-68, collapsed on one side following a gas explosion in 1968, killing five people. The explosion, four floors from the top, lifted the top four floors momentarily while the flank wall was blown out. When the load from the top four floors returned, the walls were no longer there to provide support and the floors collapsed like a house of cards.

Following the collapse, pre-fab large panel systems were abandoned, and a large number of tower blocks built that way were demolished. Hackney Council alone blew up 19 blocks. Many of the towers had already deteriorated badly. The systems had suffered from water penetration as the jointing materials aged. Poor thermal performance was also been a feature, and widespread condensation made many tenants' lives miserable. In the haste to build, and perhaps cut corners, there had also been much bad workmanship, which added to the problems of maintaining the buildings.

Councils tended to use multi-storey housing as

Below: Empress State Building, Lillie Road. Image: 1979. Courtesy of the London Metropolitan Archives.

repositories for the poorest and most deprived. Crime rates were high, encouraged by ease of escape and the general anonymity that characterised the bleak, inhospitable estates with their lack of social hubs and public spaces. The failure of the 1960s tower blocks contributed to a general reaction against Modernism.

The most successful of the high-rise residential estates was the Barbican – built on 40 acres in Cripplegate that were devastated by World War Two bombing. The 1951 City of London competition was won by Geoffrey Powell, Christof Bon and Peter Chamberlin, designers of Great Arthur House on the Golden Lane estate. Built in concrete in Brutalist style, the estate officially opened in 1969. Comprising three triangular 43-storey towers (126m), it offered high-density housing for 4,000, and over time has developed a school, arts and leisure centre, concert and conference facilities and a music and drama school. Unlike many local authority high-rise estates of its time the Barbican benefited from high quality management provided by the well-heeled City Corporation.

2.3 Commercial towers in the 1960s and 1970s

In 1956, the repeal of the London Building Act freed the LCC from height constraints. Taller buildings could now be allowed if the planners deemed them appropriate to their surroundings, and commercial developers seized the moment.

One of the first new tall office buildings was the Empress State Building in West Brompton in 1961 – London's first 100m building, with 28 storeys, designed by Stone, Toms & Partners.

Others that quickly followed in the early 1960s were the Shell Centre in Waterloo (107m, 27 storeys); Portland House in Westminster (101m, 29 storeys); London Wall (69m, 20 storeys); the London Hilton (101m, 28 storeys); Millbank Tower (118m, 32 storeys); the Economist Building (54m, 17 storeys); and New Zealand House (69m, 19 storeys) – the highest building in St James. The Royal Family objected to this as it was so close to Buckingham Palace and the height came down from the original 95m, thus destroying its proportions.

Then came Centre Point – the brainchild of developer Harry Hyams and architect Richard Seifert. Sited at the intersection of Oxford Street and Tottenham Court Road and completed in 1966, its 35 floors and 121m made Centre Point London's tallest skyscraper of the time. Slender, and built with pre-cast concrete, its unique and load-bearing honeycomb facade led the artist Eduardo Paolozzi to label it 'London's first pop art building'.

The tower created controversy from the very start. In return for Hyams' astute land assembling around the site, the LCC granted him a plot ratio of 10:1 – double

Below: Centre Point, New Oxford Street, designed by R Seifert & Partners. Image: 1967. Courtesy of RIBA Library Photographs Collection

Below: Commercial Union Building, flanked by the P & O Building. Photography: Crispin Boyle, 1982. Courtesy of RIBA Library Photographs Collection

what was allowed elsewhere, which attracted heavy criticism. Even more stigma was heaped on the tower as it stood empty for nearly 15 years. In the post *Cathy Come Home* world, it was seen as another of capitalism's unacceptable faces. Tenants began to arrive once Hyams dropped his pursuit of a single tenant occupancy, and the building's design was rewarded in 1994 with a Grade II listing.

The Aviva Tower, previously known as the Commercial Union building, on Leadenhall Street bears the clear influence of Mies van der Rohe in Gollins Melvin Ward's (GMW's) design. Built between 1968-69, it was then the second tallest building in the City, standing 118m high with 23 storeys. GMW was one of the first to suspend the floors from cantilevered steel beams coming out of the central service concrete core, which maximised floor space by doing away with support columns. This allowed the offices to be open plan. Distinctive cladding of anodized aluminium sealed the building and prevented internal over-heating. It was transformed by changing light conditions from grey to bronze.

Another landmark tall building of the period was the National Westminster Tower, or NatWest Tower, renamed Tower 42 in 1998 when Greycoat bought it from the

Left: Shell Centre seen from the north bank, designed by Sir Howard Robertson. Image: 1967. Courtesy of the London Metropolitan Archives
Centre left: Portland House, Victoria, designed by Howard Fairbairn & Partners Photography: John Maltby 1963. Courtesy of RIBA Library Photographs Collection
Bottom left: The Economist Building, designed by Alison and Peter Smithson. Photography: Bill Toomey 1964. Courtesy of RIBA Library Photographs Collection
Below: Moor House and St Alphage House, London Wall, designed by Lewis Solomon Kaye & Partners and Maurice Sanders Associates. Photography: Reginald Hugo de Burgh Galwey, 1962. Courtesy of RIBA Library Photographs Collection
Bottom: New Zealand House, Haymarket, designed by Robert Matthew Johnson-Marshall & Partners. Photography: Reginald Hugo de Burgh Galwey, 1963. Courtesy of RIBA Library Photographs Collection

View of Covent Garden looking towards Holborn, Centre Point in the middle distance.
Image: c. 1972. Courtesy of RIBA Library Photographs Collection

Right: Proposal for multi-storey buildings surrounding St Paul's Cathedral, by Joseph Emberton, 1946, never realised. Courtesy of RIBA Library Photographs Collection

Below: Tower 42, Old Broad Street, designed by Seifert & Partners. Photography: Crispin Boyle, 1981. Courtesy of RIBA Library Photographs Collection

Bottom right: Proposed Mansion House Square tower, by Mies van der Rohe (never realised) Photography: John Donat, 1983. Courtesy of RIBA Library Photographs Collection

bank (42 refers to 42 of its 47 floors being cantilevered). Designed by Richard Seifert and built between 1971-80, at 183m it was the tallest building in the UK for a decade until surpassed by the Canary Wharf tower of One Canada Square.

The author Herbert Wright, in *London High*, tells the story of how Seifert won public approval for the tower when its impact on views of St Paul's was being questioned. At a public exhibition, the architect displayed two potential schemes – one with the 183m tower and the other with two towers of 152m and 56m which combined to provide the same amount of office space as the single tower. The public vastly preferred the first.

The tower was built around a concrete core, which supported the cantilevered floors. These were designed in three separate sections, resembling the NatWest logo, though Seifert denied this was his intention. Only the levels 5 to 38 extended around the building.

The foundations had to be huge to support the 130,000 tonnes above. One hundred tonnes of steel reinforced every metre of height, making the walls 1.5m wide. New construction techniques were devised – in particular, a so-called interrupted slide method of slip-form concrete. A new form of laser technology meant that the top of the building was just one centimetre off the plans. Also ground-breaking was the internal M&E system. Plant floors were located on the 13th, 22nd and 31st floors as well as at the top of the core. And double-decker lifts were used for the first time, a significant space saving.

Not all proposed towers made it through the planning system. The Mansion House project was the last building Mies van der Rohe designed before he died in 1969. Without a building to his name in London – though many bore his imprint, van der Rohe was hired by Peter Palumbo to design a replacement for the Mappin & Webb site near the Bank of England when it became vacant in 1986. He came up with a 20-storey tower, clad in bronze glazing, set in new square.

Below: Alban Gate, 125 London Wall, designed by Terry Farrell & Partners. Photography: Kathy de Witt, 1992. Courtesy of RIBA Library Photographs Collection

The heritage lobby, with Prince Charles as its main cheerleader, attacked the proposal. The Prince's description of the design – 'a giant glass stump better suited to Chicago' – was followed by a royal allusion to Luftwaffe bombing, and amidst all the controversy, the project was eventually dropped. London lost the opportunity to host a building by one of the world's great Modernist architects, and substituted it for a Post Modern design by Stirling Wilford.

2.4 1980s and 1990s

Throughout most of the 1980s, tall buildings were out of fashion – a backlash caused by the perceived failures of the 1960s and 70s residential towers.

The deregulation of the financial markets by Prime Minister Thatcher in 1986, known as the 'Big Bang', revolutionised office building in the City of London. A tide of foreign banks swept in, requiring vast dealing floors which necessitated wide open offices and large glass windows to give natural light. Steel-frame buildings with raised floors, suspended ceilings and sophisticated building controls were the architectural order of the day.

To meet the new demand, in 1986 the City of London Corporation relaxed development controls, which led to a six-fold increase in planning permissions. In seven years, post Big Bang, nearly 50 per cent of the City's office space was modernised. Much of the new space came in the form of 'groundscrapers' such as Broadgate – with its relatively low-rise buildings and vast floor space for City trading operations. When attempting, and failing, in 2011 to have Broadgate listed Grade II, English Heritage said Broadgate Square represents 'an exemplar of commercial place making' and is both 'a triumph of urbanism [and] a special place in the financial heart of the capital.'

Alongside the groundscrapers, a number of taller offices sprung up: Minster Court (74m, 14 storeys, 1991); Alban Gate (82m, 18 storeys, 1992); 200 Aldersgate (91m, 21 storeys, 1992); and 54 Lombard St (87m, 19 storeys, 1992).

Frustrated at the complexities of building larger floorplates within the largely medieval street pattern of the City of London, Michael von Clemm, chairman and chief executive of Credit Suisse First Boston, together with developer G Ware Travelstead, saw the advantage of the generous tax breaks offered by the new London Docklands Development Corporation and the light planning regime in the Enterprise Zone in the mid to late 1980s, and pushed to create a new business district of 10 million sq ft at Canary Wharf on the Isle of Dogs, masterplanned by SOM. 'Wall Street on Water', as it was dubbed, had plot ratios of 12:1, much more than the City of London and a new set of dazzling towers was envisaged.

Travelstead's financial backers soon let him down. But the vision of a new financial centre was fulfilled by the Canadian developers Olympia & York, whose Cesar Pelli-designed One Canada Square (50 storeys and at 231m, 50m taller than Tower 42) became London's first tower over 200m when it opened in 1991. Three other nearby towers of over 80m – One Cabot Square, 25 North Colonnade, and 25 Cabot Square – came on stream at the same time.

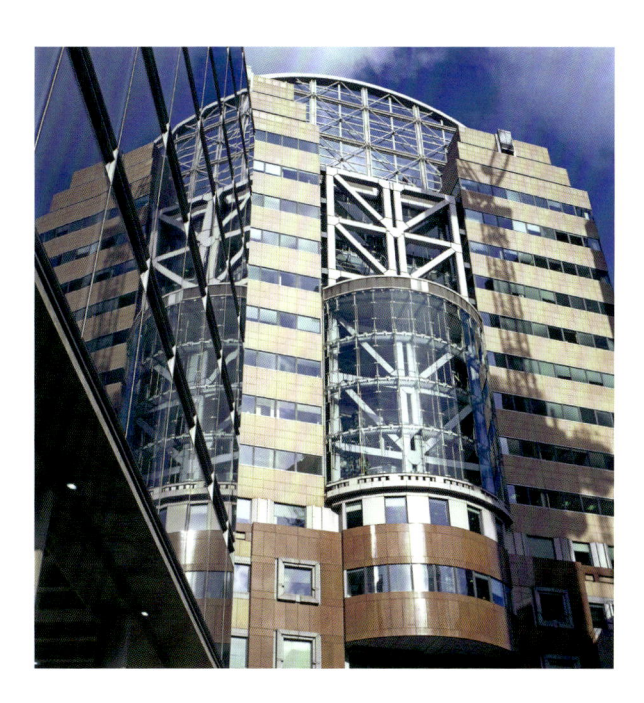

Below: Vision of the proposed Canary Wharf, by SOM c. 1987

Below: One Canada Square, designed by Cesar Pelli & Associates

One Canada Square was London's first million sq ft tower, and was built at speed, on 222 piles and a 4m thick concrete raft, and with a wind sway tolerance of 32cm from the upright. Five storeys had to be knocked off its designed height because of the proximity of London City Airport.

Recession was striking across the globe at the time, bankrupting Olympia & York the following year – another example of tall buildings' completion coinciding with an economic downturn. As property prices crashed across London there was a glut of office space to be worked through before the need arose for the next wave of towers.

2.5 2000s

By the end of the 20th century, when the Jubilee Line

Below: London Millennium tower, by Foster + Partners (never realised)

had finally reached Canary Wharf, economic recovery was firmly under way and new towers – such as One West India Quay (111m, 34 storeys, and the first in Britain to unite a hotel with luxury flats) – were under construction again.

It was at this time that the Greater London Authority (GLA) was created, and its first mayor, Ken Livingstone, was a passionate advocate of tall towers, saying: 'I have no objection in principle to London having the tallest of buildings.' His enthusiasm was in part fuelled by using Section 106 to secure funds for London regeneration from commercial development.

In *Towards the London Plan* in 2001, he stated: 'High buildings are often flagship developments that play an important part in regeneration, and they are likely to be relevant to the master planning of areas with good public transport access and capacity. A review of strategic policy relating to high buildings, including their role in maximising the density of development and their potential impact on strategic views, is being undertaken by the GLA as part of the preparation of the London Plan.'

In 2001's *Interim strategic planning guidance on tall buildings, strategic views and the skyline in London*, Livingstone continued: 'Some objectors have claimed that my policies would allow us to recreate Manhattan in London, or turn Hyde Park into Central Park with a ring of tall buildings all around. These are false claims. Policies will remain in place to protect conservation areas and strategic views although I am reviewing these policies to ensure they are not over-restrictive. In actual fact, I expect a very limited number of tall buildings to be constructed during the next decade – probably only 10-15 in all, which are likely to be located in the City of London and fringes and further East, primarily the Isle of Dogs… London must continue to grow and maintain its global pre-eminence.'

The rationale for his support was that tall buildings safeguarded and enhanced London's 'World City' role through maintaining a supply of top quality floorspace; the advantages that clusters of tall buildings can bring to London's skyline; the benefits of free-standing tall buildings in promoting regeneration and in identifying important locations; and the advantages of locating significant concentrations of new office floorspace close to existing public transport infrastructure.

Livingstone stressed that the highest architectural quality was an essential requirement in adding to London's stock of top grade buildings; in achieving exemplary public environments at ground level; and in delivering sustainable buildings that meet the most demanding

Below: 30 St Mary Axe, by Foster + Partners for Swiss Re © Nigel Young / Foster + Partners

'green' credentials. And he expressed continuing support for the conservation of the best of London's heritage.

Commenting on the prospects for tall buildings in the City of London and other areas, the GLA said in 2001: 'The market clearly indicates that Canary Wharf alone cannot meet the demand for office space in tall buildings at the present time… Office availability in central London almost halved between 1995 and 1999, with costs rising, which in turn affected business competitiveness. Without new office space, rents will continue to rise, which will impact on the profitability of London-based businesses. *Towards the London Plan* recognises a need to ensure that the future growth of office space is adequate to accommodate and enable the necessary growth. Tall office buildings will play an important role in doing this.'

In 2000, the John Prescott, deputy Prime Minister, granted planning approval for Swiss Re's plans for the first new tall building to be built in the City for 20 years, standing at 180m. This followed stalled proposals for a 386m high tower on the same site, designed by Foster + Partners, which would have been taller than the Empire State Building, twice the height of Tower 42 and still Europe's tallest tower by far (the Shard stands at 306m). The new 40-storey Foster building was supported by English Heritage with its unusual tapered shape and lozenge-shaped panes, which quickly led it to be popularly known as the 'Gherkin' (a shortened version of its original moniker of the 'Erotic Gherkin').

It was the first of the populist 'nickname' towers, which helped win public approval for it and others that have followed in more recent years such as the 'Cheesegrater' (The Leadenhall Building) and the 'Walkie Talkie' (20 Fenchurch Street) as well as two that have yet to be built, the 'Helter Skelter' (the stalled Pinnacle on Bishopsgate, thus the 'Stump') and the 'Can of Ham' (60 St Mary's Axe).

The Gherkin's tower has strong sustainability features, with natural air circulating inside the building and much natural light to cut energy bills. Rather than spoil the smooth exterior, services and equipment are located in a separate nearby six-storey glass box. Its aerodynamic shape helped reduce the strong winds that can occur at the base of some towers, and because the inner building is housed within an outer envelope, the core alone supports the vertical load.

With the Gherkin approved, new tall building proposals swiftly followed, chief among them being the Heron Tower at Bishopsgate, a one million sq ft proposal from developer Gerald Ronson and designed by KPF. At 202m tall, the plan was fiercely opposed by English Heritage because of its impact on views of St Paul's, though it had been approved by the City of London and CABE.

The ensuing public inquiry became a heavyweight battle between the pro- and anti-skyscraper brigades, and was seen at the time as a crucial test case for the future of tall buildings in London. Mayor Ken Livingstone (who wanted the tower to be higher) was backed by influential architect Richard Rogers. Their design quality argument

Below: Broadgate Tower and 201 Bishopsgate, by SOM for British Land. Photography: Christopher Hope-Finch, 2009. Courtesy of RIBA Library Photographs Collection

Below: Heron Tower, by KPF for Heron International

won the day and the Government approved the scheme in 2002. It was indeed a very significant moment for City tall buildings.

The Heron Tower's construction start was delayed until 2008, by which time the tower had grown by 28m thanks to the addition of a spire, which the City's planners were comfortable with, making it the tallest building in the Square Mile.

In the interim period, from 2005-2009, British Land's Broadgate Tower designed by SOM, was constructed. At 165m and 33 floors it marked the north edge of the Square Mile and further extended the Broadgate Estate.

In October 2004, Rogers Stirk Harbour + Partner's design for the even taller The Leadenhall Building (244m) was also accepted by English Heritage and approved by the City of London's planners. The dramatically leaning facade allowed for clear views of St Paul's from the west past towards the City. The shape constricts its footage to half the size of the biggest Canary Wharf towers.

In April 2000, property developer Irvine Sellar proposed an 87-storey, 365m cylindrical office tower at London Bridge, designed by Broadway Malyan. This was to become The Shard, now London's tallest building.

To help win approval, Sellar brought in architect Renzo Piano, Richard Rogers' partner on Pompidou Centre, who had previously described tall buildings as 'aggressive phallic fortresses'. His new elegant glass design referenced London's church spires and ships' masts. A mega piazza was to be created around London Bridge station to integrate it into the public realm. Offices occupy the lower parts of the building, with a Shangri-La Hotel taking floors 34 to 52, apartments on the next 13 floors, and a public viewing gallery.

Below: Original sketch of the Shard's design, by Renzo Piano for Sellar © Sellar Property Group

Right: The Shard viewed from the east, by Renzo Piano for Sellar © Sellar Property Group

Southwark Council approved the tower, which also significantly boosted local regeneration plans, but English Heritage and CABE opposed it on basis of its impact on views from Hampstead to St Paul's. It was called in by the Government for public inquiry, where Piano told the inspector: 'St Paul's is talking the language of stones, the other the language of glass.'. Deputy Prime Minister John Prescott took his official's advice and approved it, saying: 'For a building of this size to be acceptable, the quality of its design is critical. I am satisfied the proposed tower is of the highest quality.'

These four towers – the Gherkin, the Heron Tower, The Leadenhall Building and The Shard – indicated that using well-respected 'star architects' could help in obtaining planning approval for tall buildings. The City of London's Planning Officer Peter Rees, who played a key role at the interface between developers and the officials has said: 'Pre Big Bang, commercial office architecture was the pits.' It was he who encouraged developers to use some of the world's greatest architects, with mostly successful results.

Rees himself pays tribute to the influence of the Mayor: 'Ken Livingstone was a key figure. He recognised that London was growing, and was constrained by the Green Belt. Densification was totally logical. And he also wanted to show that London was capable of competing on the global stage. Ken recognised that tall buildings were great brand marketing for London. He wanted The Shard and the Gherkin because of the glitz and glamour they project. They're a great billboard for the City.' It was Ken Livingstone who first introduced the London View Management Framework in 2007, which identified 26 strategically important views for London. This updated on previous regional planning guidance on strategic views, which protected 10 views of London first identified in 1991.

When Boris Johnson was elected Mayor in 2008, however, he postured concern for the impact of new tall towers on London's heritage, and acted to have London's viewing corridors widened to protect key views of historic landmarks. In his housing manifesto Building a Better London he said: 'London's skyline is precious. Tall buildings must be part of London's development, but not at the expense of existing landmarks. Tourists flock to London because of its landmarks, and 91% of people want views protected around St Paul's and the Palace of Westminster.'

Although their politics differed on this policy, Mayor Johnson too has grasped the importance of tall buildings to project London's global pre-eminence, and has similarly seen the benefits of using developer cash to aid inner-city regeneration.

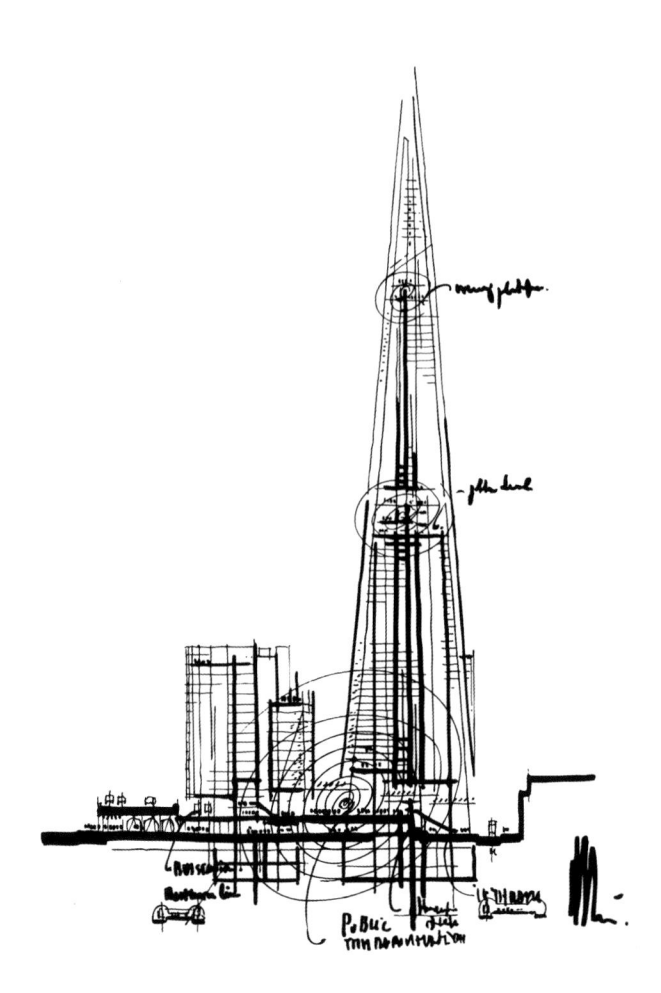

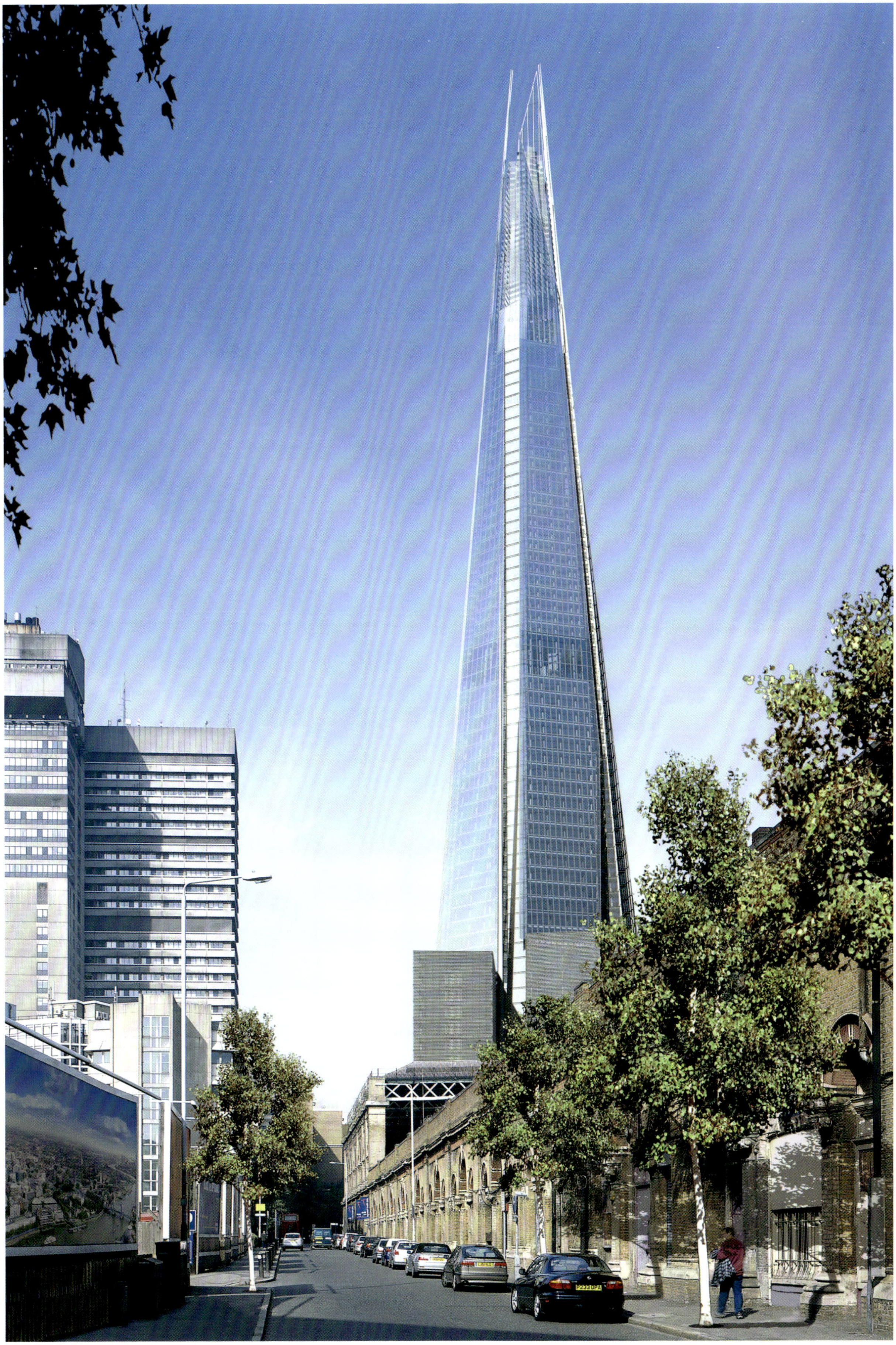

Pinnacle of 30 St Mary Axe with Canary Wharf in the background. Photography: Luke Palmer, 2008. Courtesy of RIBA Library Photographs Collection

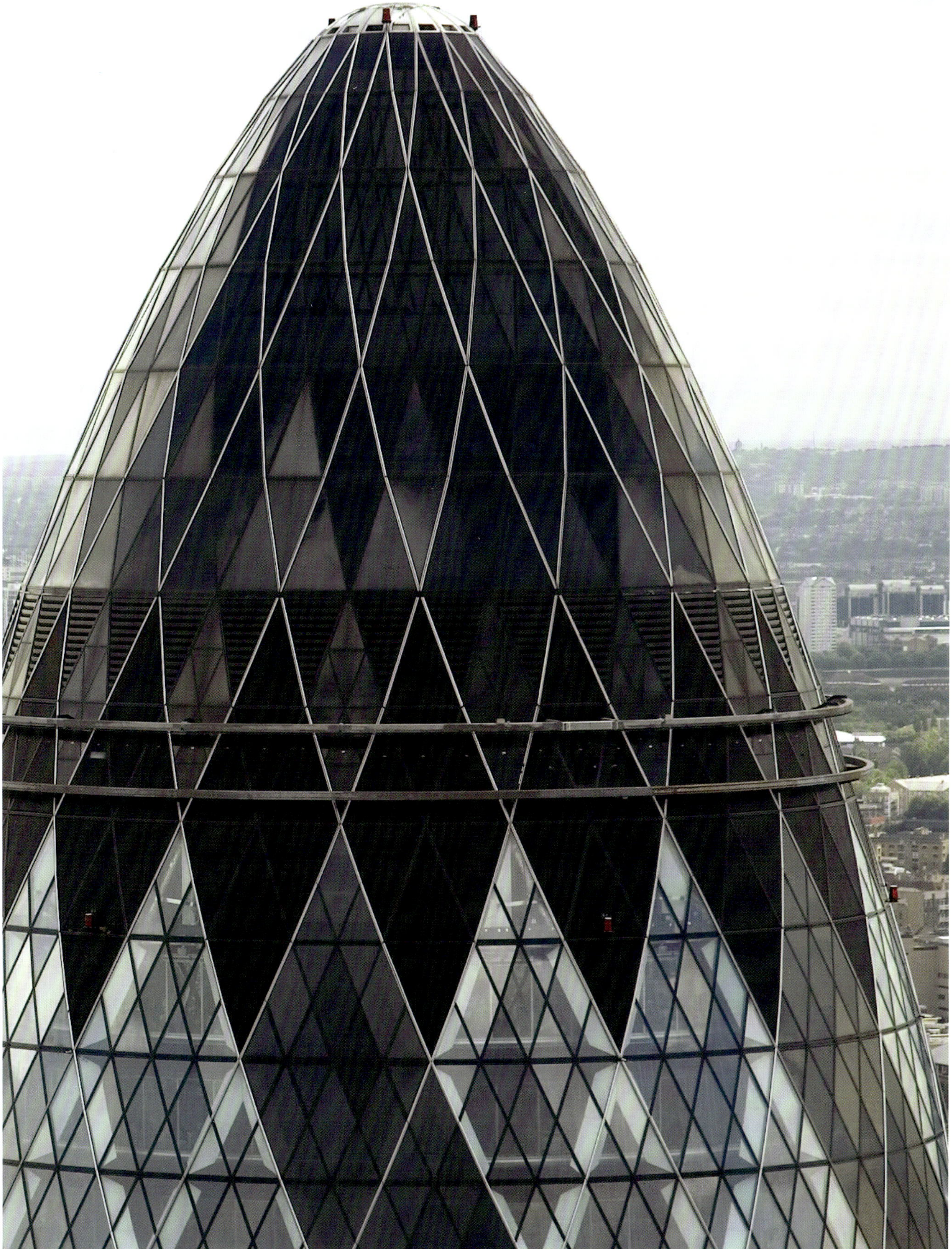

CHAPTER 3
The current wave of tall towers

London today is seeing a new wave of tall buildings entering the development pipeline which, if all complete, will dramatically alter the skyline of the capital over the next decade.

NLA have partnered with property consultants GL Hearn to undertake a bespoke research project on tall building proposals across Greater London, in order to understand the scale of development proposed, the findings of which been analysed by GL Hearn. Tall buildings have been defined as those of 20 storeys or more, and the analysis has considered towers that are proposed (without planning permission), approved (with planning permission) or under construction (but not yet completed). For a small number of proposed towers it has not been possible to establish the current status.

To understand Londoners' views on this scale of development and how far perceptions about tall buildings have changed since the completion of structures such as The Shard and The Gherkin, NLA have also conducted a London-wide survey with Ipsos Mori, the results of which are in section 3.5.

3.1 Numbers, height and status

The research has shown that there are a total of 236 towers in the pipeline across London. As detailed in **Table 1 and Figure 1** on the next page, close to half of the pipeline towers already have planning permission (113 / 48%) but have not yet been commenced and some 45 (or 19%) of towers are currently under construction. There are 72 (30%) towers in the pipeline without planning permission and 6 (3%) proposals where the status could not be confirmed.

The analysis assessed proposals above 20 storeys – the tallest proposed tower is the Pinnacle in the City of London, a commercial tower, standing at 288m (60 storeys). The towers with the highest numbers of storeys are residential; City Pride, Columbus Tower, Quay House and South Quay Plaza, all of which would extend to 75 storeys.

Table 2 and Figure 2 shows all of the proposed towers by number of storeys – storey heights and overall tower heights will vary between developments as a result of design and use.

Approximately 57% of the pipeline towers are between 20 and 29 storeys with just 10% extending above 50 storeys. The figures suggest that towers are feasible at any height up to the current maximum of 75 storeys.

Table 1: Status of Tall Buildings Reviewed (Source: NLA / GL Hearn)

Status	Number Of Tall Buildings	% of Tall Buildings Reviewed
Approved	113	48
Proposed	72	31
Status Unknown	6	3
Under Construction	45	19
Total	**236**	**100**

Figure 1: Comparison between the Status of Tall Buildings Reviewed
(Source: NLA / GL Hearn)

Status	Number of tall buildings	% of tall buildings reviewed
Approved	113	48
Proposed	72	31
Status Unknown	6	3
Under Construction	45	19

Table 2: Storey Heights of Tall Buildings Reviewed (Source: NLA / GL Hearn)

Storeys	No. Of Tall Buildings	% of Tall Buildings Reviewed
20 - 29	134	57
30 - 39	47	20
40 - 49	33	14
50 - 59	16	7
60+	6	3
Total	**236**	**100**

Figure 2: Height of Tall Buildings Reviewed (Source: NLA / GL Hearn)

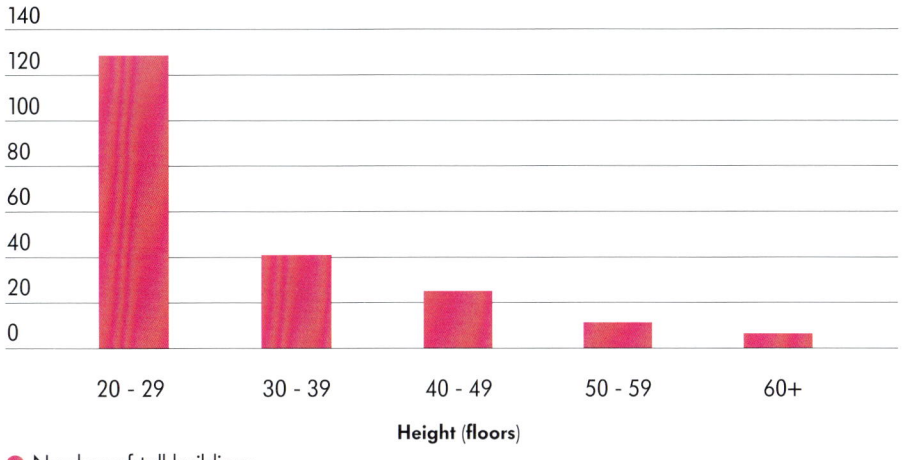

● Number of tall buildings

3.2 Location

Table 3 and Figure 3 show the geographic distribution of towers by borough. Whilst there are tall building proposals across London, certain boroughs are set to accommodate far higher numbers of towers than others. This may be expected to some extent given the varying planning opportunities and constraints across London allied to local economic and market factors. The figures are nevertheless striking in that more than 36% of towers are proposed in just two boroughs (Tower Hamlets and Southwark) – almost one quarter of all tall building proposals in London are in Tower Hamlets alone (55 / 23%).

The dominance of Tower Hamlets is reflected in the status tall building proposals (**Table 6**) – the borough has the most approved towers (22 or 19%) and the most proposed towers (14 or 19%). Tower Hamlets also has the highest number development projects under construction with 13 proposals (29%).

The emerging importance and significance of the Southbank as a tall building location is highlighted by a total of 37 (51%) of proposed tall buildings in Greenwich, Southwark, Lambeth and Wandsworth.

The amount of tower development in the Central, South and East sub-regions (**Table 4 and Figure 4**) is very evident with these sub-regions accounting for 204 of proposals in the pipeline (87%). Accordingly, the very small number of tall buildings proposed in the North and West sub-regions is striking given the geographic extent and nature of these sub-regions; just 22 (9%) and 10 (4%) respectively. By way of example, Ealing, Hounslow and Camden have only 1 proposal in each borough. Whilst many locations in these sub-regions will not be suitable for tall buildings, there are areas of lower density uses that are suitable for regeneration and the potential for taller buildings. It is likely that the number of proposals in these sub regions will increase as Opportunity Areas move forward towards to delivery.

Table 3: Total Number / Percentage of Tall Buildings Reviewed Per London Borough (Source: NLA / GL Hearn)

Borough	Total no. of Tall Buildings	% of Tall Buildings Reviewed
Barking & Dagenham	3	1.27
Barnet	20	8.47
Brent	4	1.69
Camden	1	0.42
City of London	8	3.39
Croydon	10	4.24
Ealing	1	0.42
Greenwich	18	7.63
Hackney	7	2.97
Hammersmith & Fulham	4	1.69
Haringey	2	0.85
Hounslow	1	0.42
Islington	9	3.81
Kensington and Chelsea	2	0.85
Kensington and Chelsea / Hammersmith & Fulham	2	0.85
Lambeth	31	13.14
Lewisham	8	3.39
Newham	16	6.78
Southwark	20	8.47
Tower Hamlets	55	23.31
Wandsworth	11	4.66
Westminster	3	1.27
Total	**236**	**100.00**

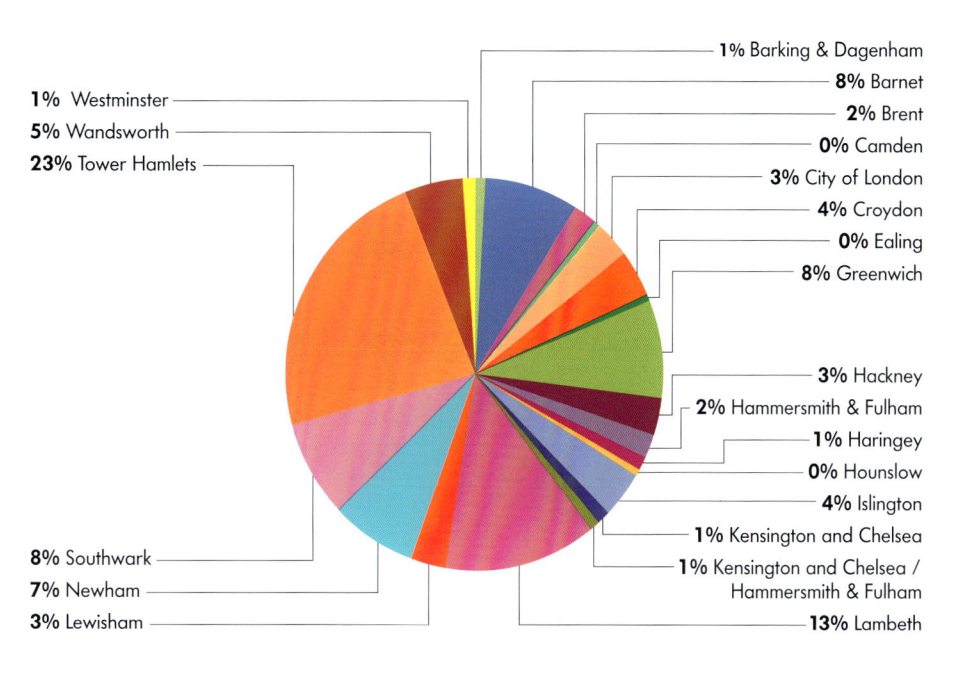

Figure 3: Percentage of Tall Buildings Per London Borough
(Source: NLA / GL Hearn)

- 1% Barking & Dagenham
- 8% Barnet
- 2% Brent
- 0% Camden
- 3% City of London
- 4% Croydon
- 0% Ealing
- 8% Greenwich
- 3% Hackney
- 2% Hammersmith & Fulham
- 1% Haringey
- 0% Hounslow
- 4% Islington
- 1% Kensington and Chelsea
- 1% Kensington and Chelsea / Hammersmith & Fulham
- 13% Lambeth
- 3% Lewisham
- 7% Newham
- 8% Southwark
- 23% Tower Hamlets
- 5% Wandsworth
- 1% Westminster

Table 4: Number / Percentage Of Tall Buildings Per London Sub-Region
(Source: NLA / GL Hearn)

London Sub-Region	No. Of Tall Buildings	% of Tall Buildings Studied
North	22	9
West	10	4
South	21	9
East	107	45
Central	76	32
Total	**236**	**100**

Figure 4: Comparison between the numbers of Tall Buildings Per London Sub-Region (Source: NLA / GL Hearn)

London sub-region	Number of tall buildings
North	22
West	10
South	21
East	107
Central	76

Table 5: Primary Uses of Tall Buildings Reviewed (Source: NLA / GL Hearn)

Primary Use	Number Of Tall Buildings	% Of Tall Buildings
Commercial	7	3.0
Hotel	8	3.4
Mixed Use	13	5.5
Office	18	7.6
Residential	189	80.1
University	1	0.4
Total	**236**	**100.0**

Figure 5: Comparison of the Primary Use of Tall Buildings Reviewed
(Source: NLA / GL Hearn)

Primary use	Number of tall buildings
Commercial	7
Hotel	8
Mixed-use	13
Office	18
Residential	189
University	1

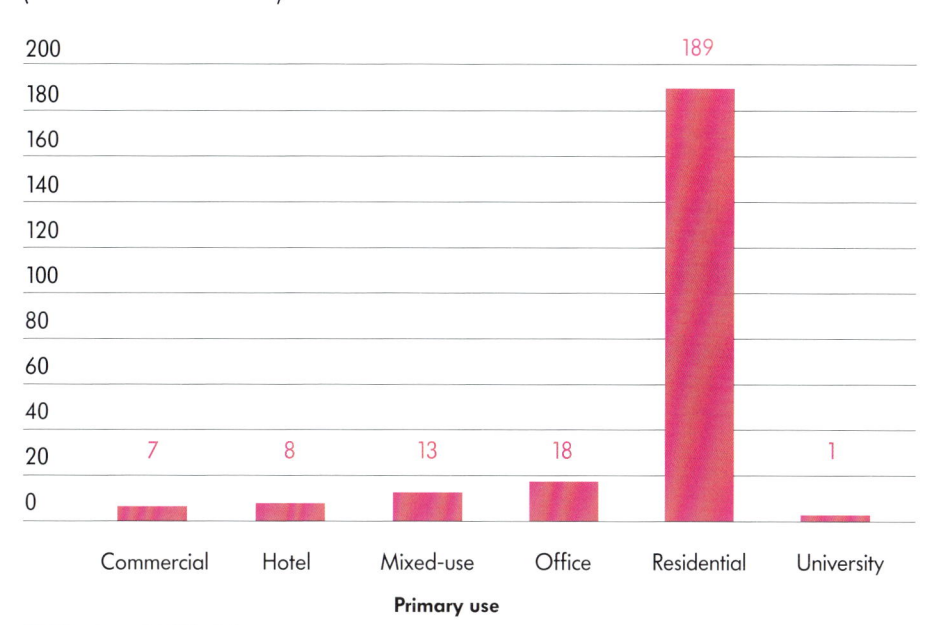

Table 6: Status of Tall Buildings Per London Borough (Source: NLA / GL Hearn)

Borough	Approved	Proposed	Status Unknown	Under Construction	Total
Barking & Dagenham	3	0	0	0	3
Barnet	20	0	0	0	20
Brent	4	0	0	0	4
Camden	1	0	0	0	1
City of London	4	1	0	3	8
Croydon	5	3	0	2	10
Ealing	1	0	0	0	1
Greenwich	8	10	0	0	18
Hackney	5	0	0	2	7
Hammersmith & Fulham	3	1	0	0	4
Haringey	1	1	0	0	2
Hounslow	0	0	0	1	1
Islington	1	4	0	4	9
Kensington and Chelsea	0	2	0	0	2
Kensington and Chelsea / Hammersmith & Fulham	0	0	0	2	2
Lambeth	14	11	0	6	31
Lewisham	5	3	0	0	8
Newham	8	5	0	3	16
Southwark	5	8	0	7	20
Tower Hamlets	22	14	6	13	55
Wandsworth	2	8	0	1	11
Westminster	1	1	0	1	3
Total					**236**

3.3 Type and use

Table 5 and Figure 5 summarises the primary use of the tall buildings assessed. Unsurprisingly, in current market conditions, the vast majority of towers are proposed for residential development (189 or 80%). This is clearly a response to the strength in the residential market, allied to high levels of demand, housing targets and limited land supply. Of commercial uses, office towers are most prevalent (18 / 8%) and there are 8 (3%) proposals where the primary use is hotel. University/educational use are notable in that there is only 1 tall building proposed for these uses.

3.4 Key findings

The research has identified 236 tall building proposals across London – it has focused on buildings above 20 storeys, but in many instances buildings below that threshold will still be considered to be 'tall' in the local context. Of the total pipeline, approximately half of the proposals have planning permission, with 45 schemes already under construction. There is no particular discernible trend in terms of height, but the majority of proposals are between 20-29 storeys (134 / 57%). Tower Hamlets is by far away the most populous location for tall buildings in terms of towers that are proposed, approved and under construction.

There are marked geographic patterns at the sub-regional scale as well. London Plan Opportunity Areas are located across the capital, but the predominance of the Central, South and East sub-regions – in stark contrast to the North and West – is very marked in terms of tall building proposals.

It is no surprise that the tall building proposals are predominantly residential as a result of planning, economic and market conditions representing a distinct phase of tower planning in London. Planning permissions are in place for the new wave of tall buildings, and delivery has started in a new phase of London's growth and development. Tall building proposals are complex and thoroughly tested in terms of design and potential impacts; the success of the planning system should be judged on the quality of these new buildings and neighbourhoods, as they rapidly emerge across the city.

3.5 Public perceptions

In February 2014 NLA and Ipsos MORI conducted a survey into Londoners' views on tall buildings in the capital, defined as buildings over 20 storeys high. 500 people from across London gave us their views.

53% of Londoners said that whether a tall tower looks right in relation to its surroundings should be given highest priority when deciding whether or not it should be built in London. Whether it has a good design was next priority at **35%**, while only **11%** said that how tall it is should be the most important factor

Only **27%** of Londoners would be happy to live in a tall building, while **60%** of Londoners would be happy to work in a tall building

46% of Londoners agree that tall buildings have made London look better, **25%** disagree

The Gherkin at **36%** and The Shard at **22%** were chosen as the towers Londoners liked best when asked to select from a list of 13 tall buildings

When asked whether they believe there are currently too many tall towers in London, – **40%** disagreed with the statement, while **32%** agreed

Over the next 5 years, **37%** of Londoners would like to see fewer new tall buildings than were built in the last 5 years, **33%** would like to see about the same number, and **26%** would like to see more

31% of Londoners agree that enough is done to control the number of tall buildings built in London, **26%** disagree

Ipsos MORI interviewed a representative sample of 500 members of the public aged 16-64. Interviews were carried out online between 14-18 February 2014. Data are weighted to be representative of the population. Full question text, and detailed tables are available at www.ipsos-mori.com

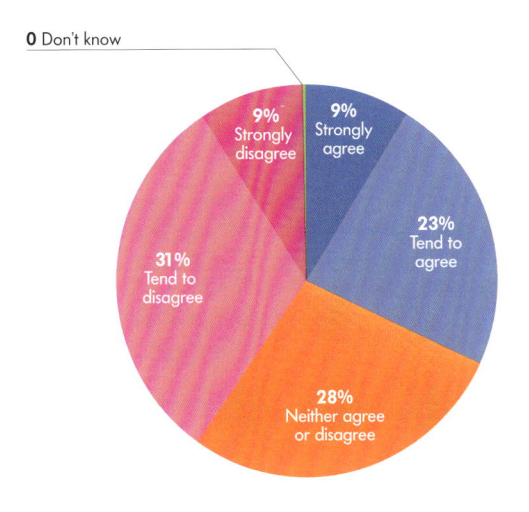

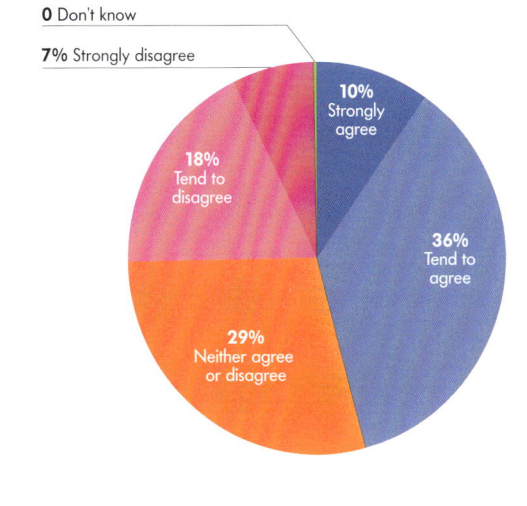

There are too many tall buildings in London

- 0 Don't know
- 9% Strongly disagree
- 9% Strongly agree
- 23% Tend to agree
- 28% Neither agree or disagree
- 31% Tend to disagree

Tall buildings have made London look better

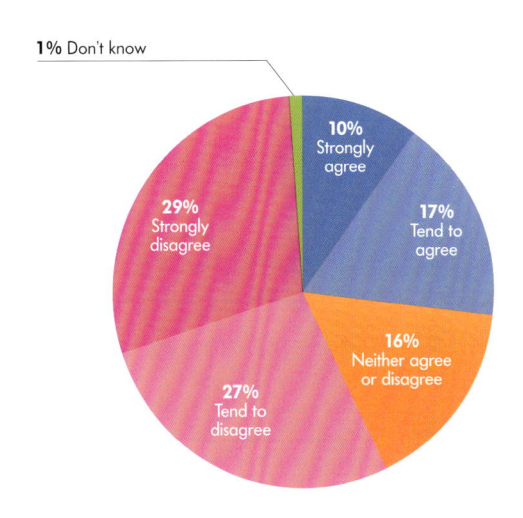

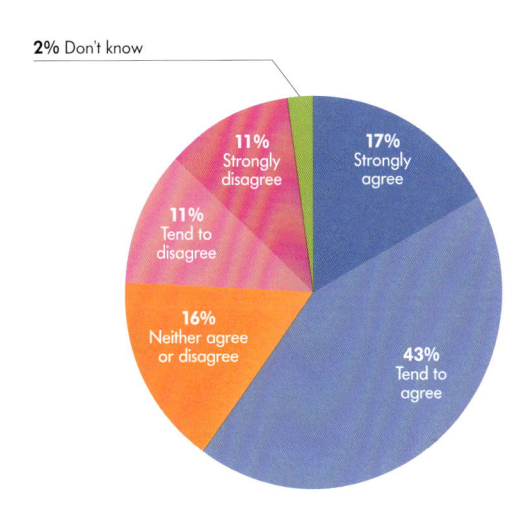

- 0 Don't know
- 7% Strongly disagree
- 10% Strongly agree
- 36% Tend to agree
- 29% Neither agree or disagree
- 18% Tend to disagree

I would be happy living in a tall building

- 1% Don't know
- 10% Strongly agree
- 17% Tend to agree
- 16% Neither agree or disagree
- 27% Tend to disagree
- 29% Strongly disagree

I would be happy working in a tall building

- 2% Don't know
- 17% Strongly agree
- 43% Tend to agree
- 16% Neither agree or disagree
- 11% Tend to disagree
- 11% Strongly disagree

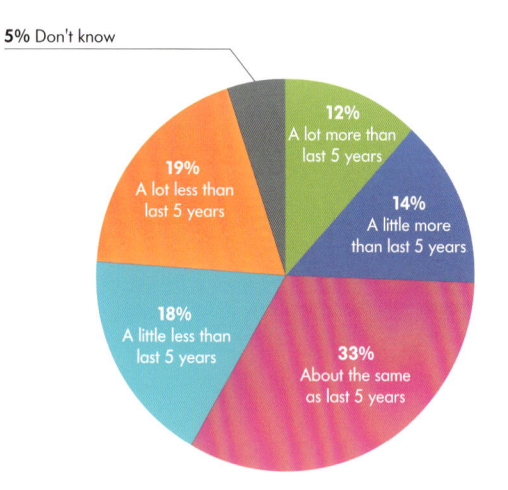

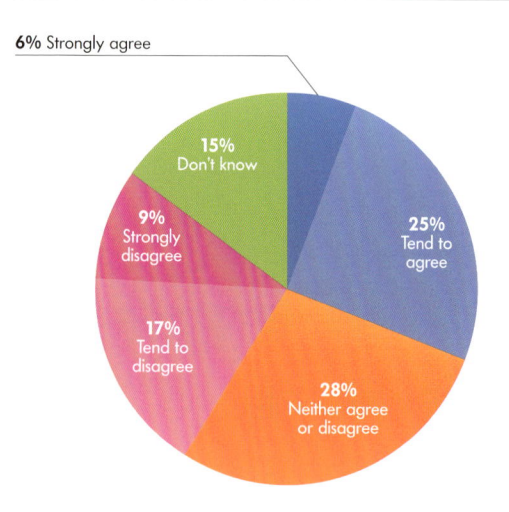

Chart 1:
- 5% Don't know
- 12% A lot more than last 5 years
- 14% A little more than last 5 years
- 33% About the same as last 5 years
- 18% A little less than last 5 years
- 19% A lot less than last 5 years

Thinking about the next 5 years, which, if any, of these best describes your view about how many new tall buildings should be allowed to be built in London?

Chart 2:
- 6% Strongly agree
- 25% Tend to agree
- 28% Neither agree or disagree
- 17% Tend to disagree
- 9% Strongly disagree
- 15% Don't know

To what extent do you agree or disagree that enough is done to control how many tall buildings over 20-storeys are being built in London?

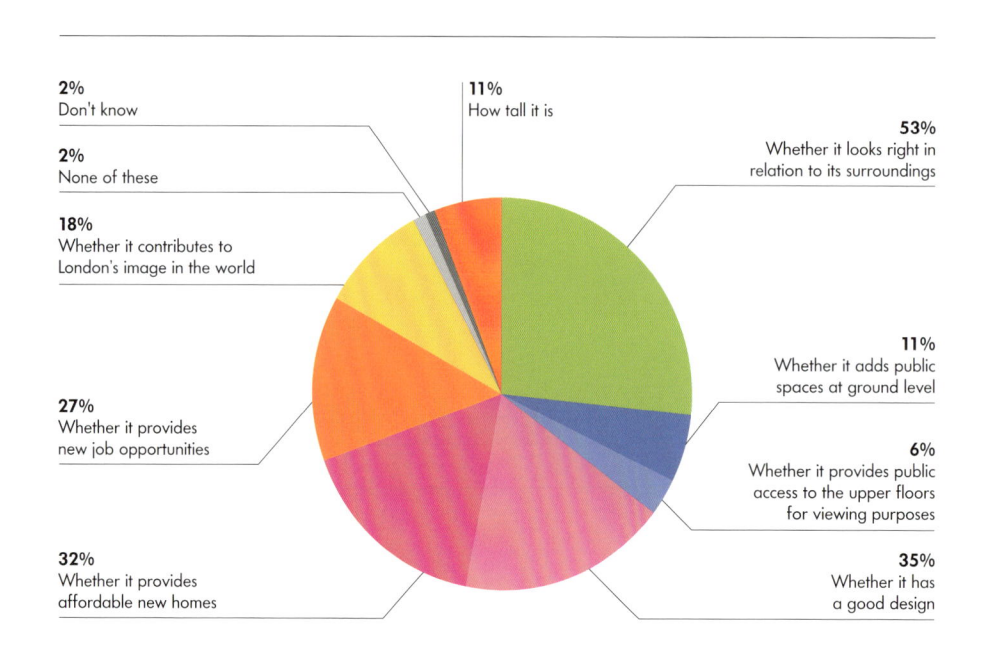

Chart 3:
- 2% Don't know
- 2% None of these
- 18% Whether it contributes to London's image in the world
- 27% Whether it provides new job opportunities
- 32% Whether it provides affordable new homes
- 11% How tall it is
- 53% Whether it looks right in relation to its surroundings
- 11% Whether it adds public spaces at ground level
- 6% Whether it provides public access to the upper floors for viewing purposes
- 35% Whether it has a good design

Which of these factors should be given highest or second highest priority by those deciding whether or not a new tall building should be built in London?

66 LONDON'S GROWING UP!

Which of these tall buildings do you like best?

30 St Mary Axe	**36%**
The Shard	**22%**
The Leadenhall Building	**8%**
One Canada Square	**8%**
Strata Tower	**6%**
St George Wharf	**4%**
20 Fenchurch Street	**4%**
Tower 42	**1%**
Broadgate Tower	**1%**
Centre Point	**1%**
St Helen's	**1%**
The Heron Tower	**1%**
Barbican	**0%**
None of these	**5%**
Don't know	**1%**

Future view from Parliament Hill
© Hayes Davidson

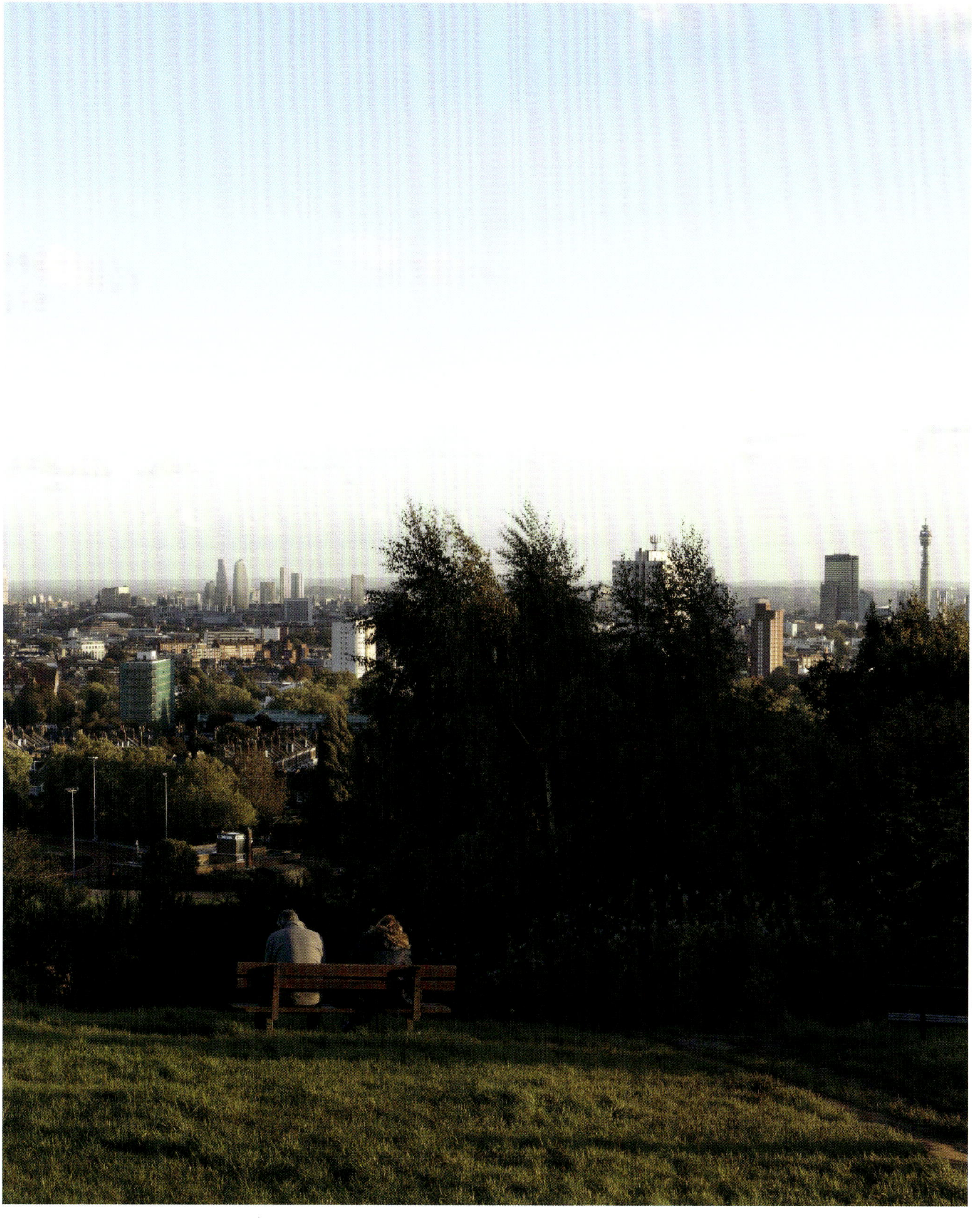

CHAPTER 4
Key areas of growth

4.1 Vauxhall Nine Elms

Vauxhall Nine Elms is one of the most significant central London regeneration zones in the city. Straddling the boundaries of the boroughs of Lambeth and Wandsworth, it stretches roughly from Battersea Power Station to Lambeth Bridge and covers around 195 acres. Traditionally a largely derelict industrial district, a major redevelopment programme is breathing new life into the area to include more than 18,000 new homes, a £1 billion extension to the Northern Line and two new tube stations; £45 million improvements to the Vauxhall tube station; remodeling of the gyratory at Vauxhall; new schools; and approximately 50 acres of new public space.

The site represents a significant opportunity to develop new homes and jobs on a large central London site and as such there is intense pressure for fairly high-density development. An Opportunity Area Planning Framework (OAPF) for the area, developed by the GLA in partnership with Lambeth and Wandsworth Councils, TfL and English Heritage, includes a tall building strategy in order to establish a set of parameters which respond to the need to protect key views as set out in the LVMF and to encourage high-density development in the form of 8-10 storey perimeter blocks in certain locations.

The Framework supports an emerging tall building cluster at Vauxhall, defined as a series of tall buildings coming forward as separate individual elements on the skyline to a maximum of 150m, with the pinnacle being formed by the Vauxhall Tower at 180m. Further west, at Albert Embankment, tall buildings should be no more than 80-90m in height and should 'avoid appearing cumulatively as a uniform wall of development in strategic views from Waterloo, Hungerford and Westminster bridges', while at Nine Elms and Battersea, tall buildings should be no more than 60-70m in height.

Examples of tall buildings include:
– One Nine Elms: Designed by KPF these two towers of 43 storeys and 58 storeys will stand at 161m and 200m once completed in 2016, and include a mix of residential, offices and retail. The development occupies a prominent position in the emerging tall building cluster in Vauxhall, and the height of the tallest tower currently exceeds the peak defined in the OAPF for Vauxhall. Planning permission for the development was granted in 2012. The development has been bought by Chinese investment and development conglomerate Dalian Wanda Group.
– The Tower at One St George Wharf: This is one of the first tall buildings to have completed in the area, standing at 180m and 53 storeys, and provides 213 luxury apartments. Designed by Broadway Malyan, it is currently the highest residential tower in UK. Occupying a prominent position on the river, the scheme went to public inquiry in 2005 because of its height and proximity to the Palace of Westminster but was approved by Deputy Prime Minister John Prescott.
– Sainsbury's Nine Elms: The redevelopment of the Sainsbury's site has been designed to deliver a larger Sainsbury's store, 737 homes, business and retail space and the site for a new Northern Line extension. Three towers designed by Rolfe Judd Architects – residential buildings ranging up to 129m – are roughly positioned on each corner of the triangular site with the tallest building furthest to the east and a new public square.

Right: Current view of Vauxhall Nine Elms from Lambeth Bridge
© Hayes Davidson
Below: Projected view of Vauxhall Nine Elms from Lambeth Bridge
© Hayes Davidson

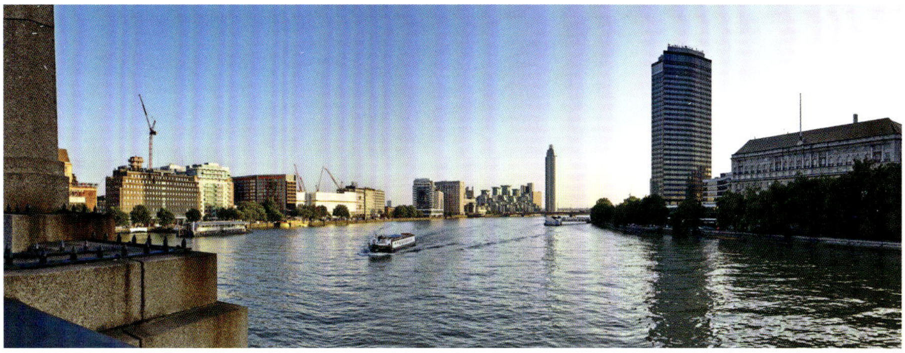

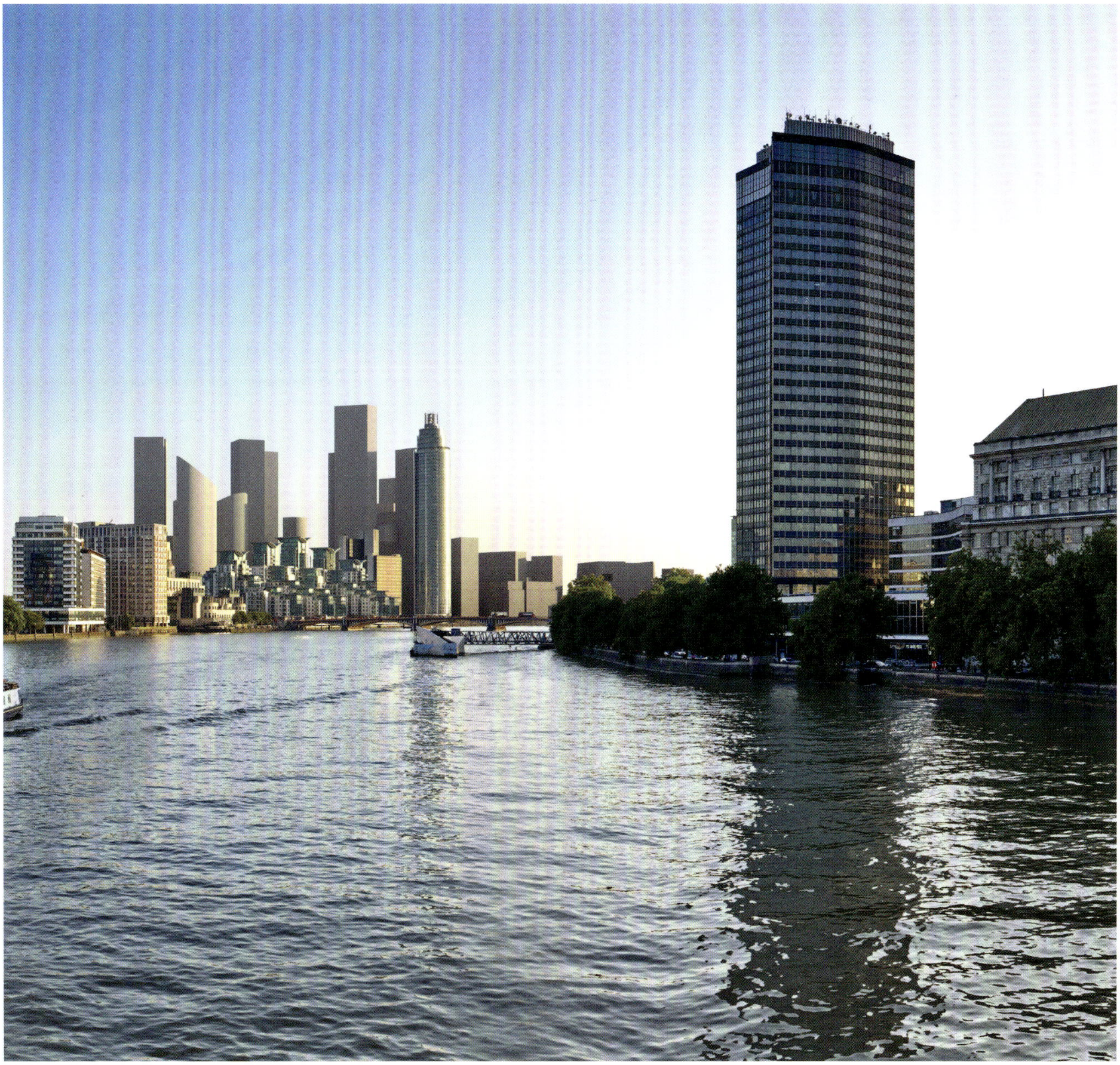

Right: Current view of Vauxhall
Nine Elms from Millbank
© Hayes Davidson
Below: Projected view of
Vauxhall Nine Elms from Millbank
© Hayes Davidson

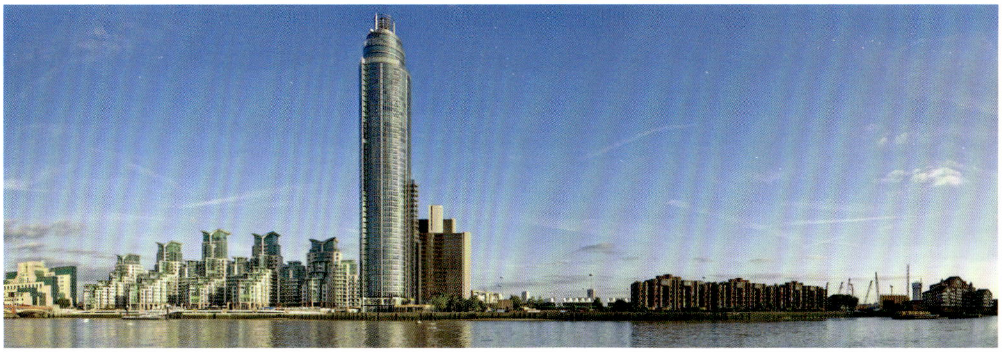

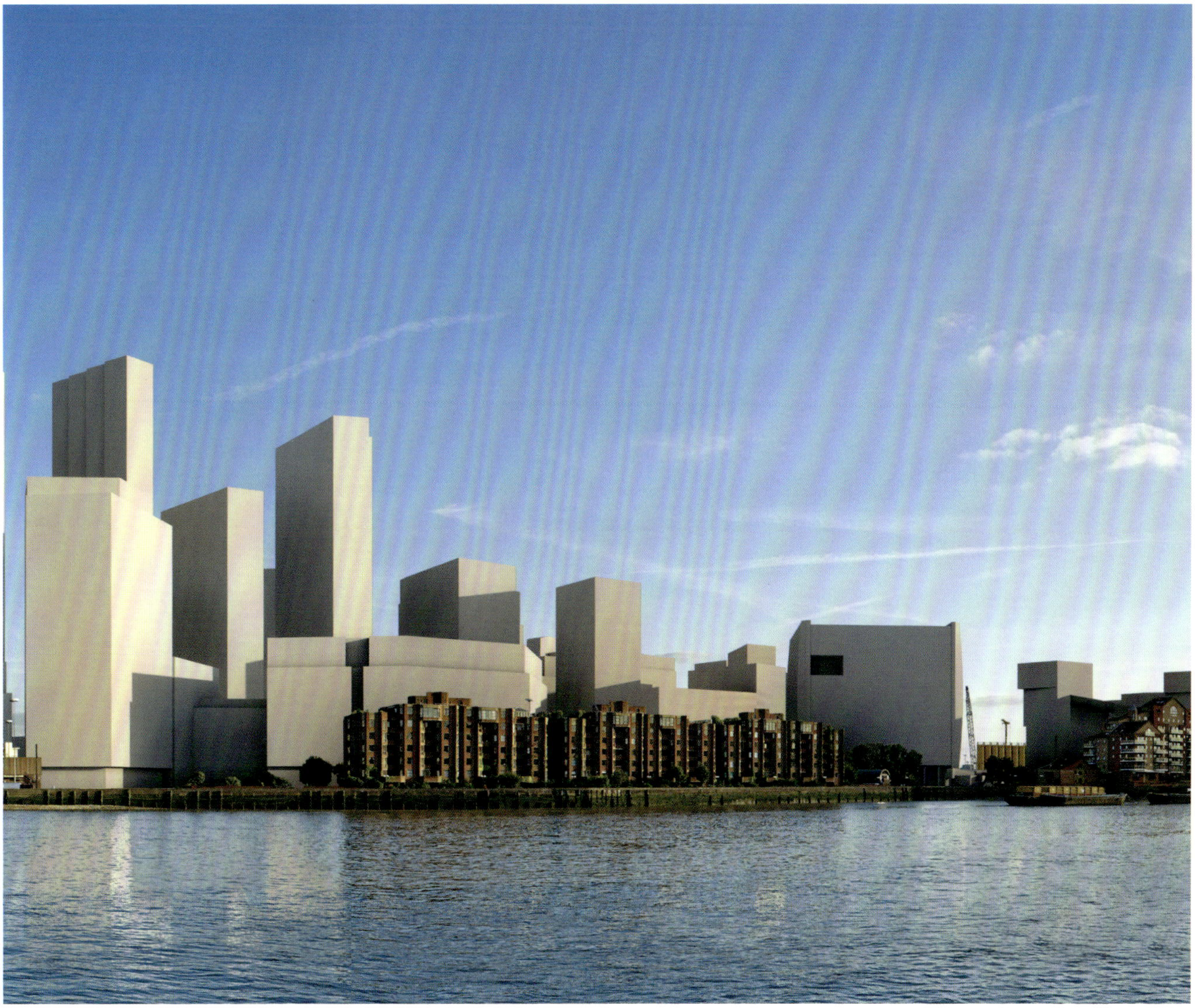

Left: Vauxhall Nine Elms Opportunity Area masterplan, 2012, courtesy of the GLA
Below: View from Waterloo Bridge showing proposed development heights, 2012, courtesy of GLA
Bottom: Proposed development heights in Vauxhall Nine Elms, 2012, courtesy of the GLA

Albert Embankment | Vauxhall | Nine Elms | Battersea
Existing situation

Buildings up to 80-90m high | 150m indicative threshold | Vauxhall Tower Pinnacle 180m | Buildings up to 60-70m high
Hampton House
Albert Embankment | Vauxhall | Nine Elms | Battersea
Height parameters

Albert Embankment | Vauxhall | Nine Elms | Battersea
Potential skyline

76 LONDON'S GROWING UP!

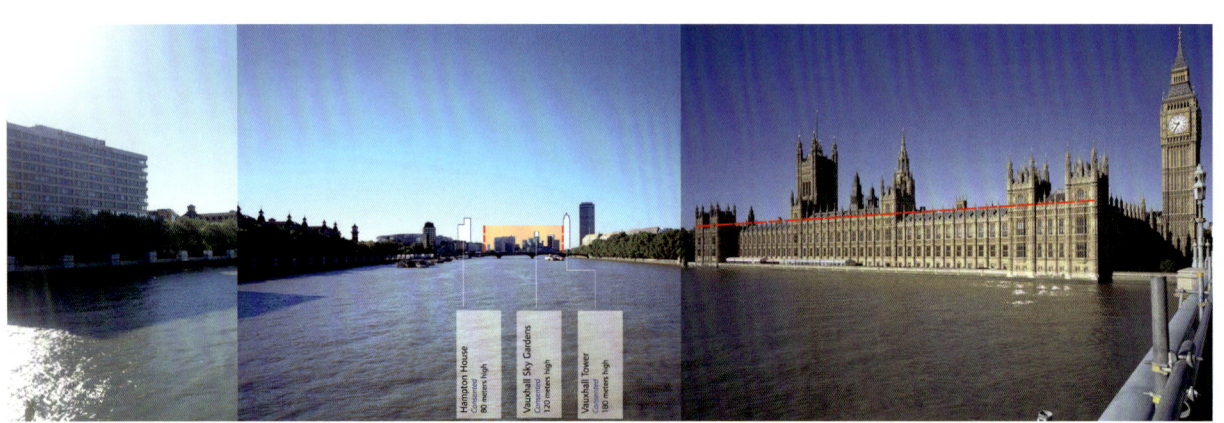

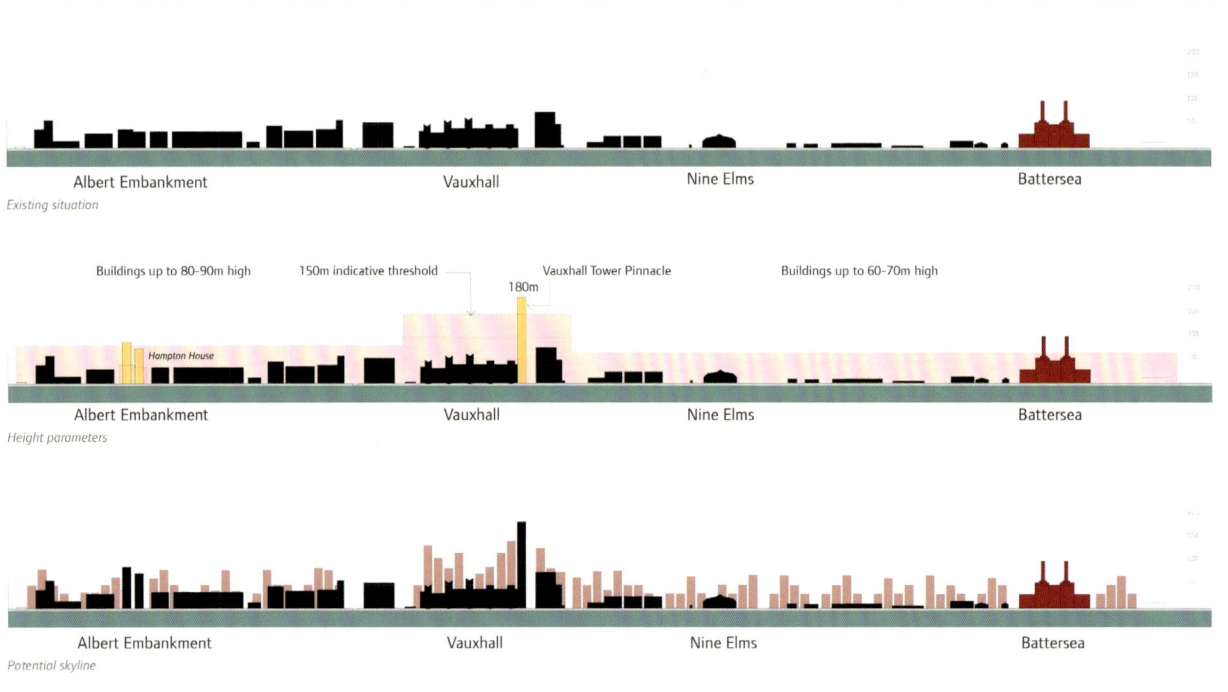

Below: One Nine Elms, by KPF for Dalian Wanda (proposed) ©ATCHAIN and KPF
Bottom: One Nine Elms and surrounds (proposed) ©ATCHAIN and KPF

Below: The Tower, One St George Wharf, by Broadway Malyan for St George London Ltd

Below: Tall building strategy for Elephant and Castle, view from south, 2012, courtesy of Southwark Council.

4.2 Elephant and Castle

The Elephant and Castle Opportunity Area in Southwark covers an area of 122 hectares. Southwark Council is aiming to stimulate 440,000 sqm of new development with up to 45,000 sqm of new shopping and leisure floor space and 25,000-30,000 sqm of business floorspace. It has a target of 4,000 new homes and a minimum of 1,400 affordable housing units. Developers Lend Lease are leading on a major transformation of the area.

A Supplementary Planning Document (SPD) for the area stresses that tall buildings will help to signal its regeneration and that the tallest buildings should act as focal points in views towards the Elephant and Castle along main roads and strengthen gateways in the central area. Moving away from the tallest points, buildings should diminish in height to manage the transition down to the existing context. The council says they are to be used to add interest to London's skyline and when viewed in a cluster, should be articulated to ensure that they do not coalesce to form a single mass.

The 148m Strata Tower, London's tallest residential building until The Tower at One St George Wharf completed in 2013, was completed in June 2010. New towers emerging in the area include:

– One the Elephant, a 37-storey residential development designed by Squire and Partners for Lend Lease, which is currently under construction and due to complete in 2015.
– '360 London' or 'Newington Butts' – a 45-storey tower designed by Rogers Stirk Harbour + Partners which will contain a significant number of private rented units.
– Eileen House, a 41-storey residential tower at the northern edge of the site. The scheme had been opposed by Ministry of Sound next door, for fear that noise complaints from the new residents would lead to its closure. The original scheme by Oakmaye Properties was originally rejected by Southwark Council; however it was 'called in' by the Mayor and approved in 2014 with a number of conditions to ensure noise mitigation.

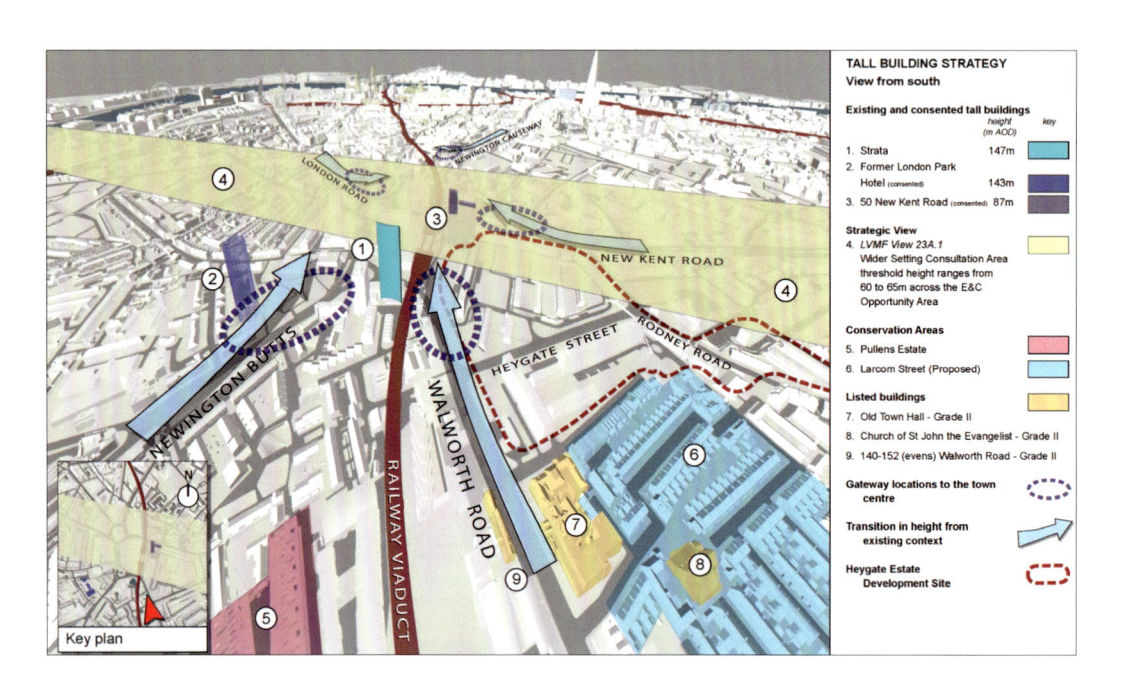

Below: Strata Tower, by BFLS for Brookfield Europe. Photography: Agnese Sanvito
Bottom: Aerial view of the future Elephant and Castle quarter, courtesy of Southwark Council.

Below: Newington Butts, by Rogers Stirk Harbour + Partners for Mace / Essential Living (proposed)

4.3 Blackfriars Road

Blackfriars Road is a wide boulevard running south from the River Thames to historic St George's Circus, forming part of the 'Blackfriars Mile', linking Elephant and Castle to the South Bank and beyond to the City. The area is being transformed by a series of new high-rise developments alongside the opening of a new entrance to Blackfriars Station and public realm schemes.

The Blackfriars Road SPD sets out that tall buildings are encouraged where they reinforce the character and function of this main route into central London. The tallest buildings should be at the north end of the road, signifying the gateway to central London and the gateway to Southwark. The SPD also encourages tall buildings of a height of up to 70m at Southwark tube station and at the southern end of Blackfriars Road towards St George's Circus to provide a focal point. Any buildings over 50m must demonstrate that they contribute positively to London's skyline and make 'exceptional contribution to the regeneration of the area'.

– One Blackfriars: Architect Ian Simpson's design for developer St George has been nicknamed the 'Boomerang' thanks to its curved southern side that has been planned to maintain views of The Shard from around Waterloo Bridge. Standing at 170m, it will provide a mix of residential, hotel and retail uses. In lieu of affordable housing on site, the developer will be contributing £29 million to Southwark Council. The council intends to construct housing on a less expensive site and build a greater number of affordable units as a result.
– Ludgate and Sampson House: Standing opposite One Blackfriars is a £1 billion regeneration scheme designed by PLP Architecture for private equity firm The Carlyle Group, for which Southwark Council gave a resolution to grant planning permission in late 2013. The development consists of nine new buildings on the site, ranging in height from five to 48 storeys (up to 170m). The scheme, to be completed in 2023, will create 492 homes and 300,000 sq ft of offices while Carlyle is also paying £75 million in Section 106 to the council, including £65 million for affordable homes off-site. As well as building a new public square, the developer will improve accessibility to the Thames and reopen parts of the Upper Ground thoroughfare for the first time in 150 years.
– 240 Blackfriars Road: This is a 20-storey predominantly commercial tower designed by Allford Hall Monaghan Morris (AHMM) for the Great Ropemaker Partnership and is currently nearing completion. Media and publishing company UBM has taken a 105,000 sq ft pre-let to function as its UK headquarters.

Bottom: Sampson House and Ludgate House by PLP Architecture for The Carlyle Group and One Blackfriars by Ian Simpson Architects for St George South London (proposed)

Right: 240 Blackfriars by AHMM for Great Ropemaker Partnership
Below: Aerial view of future approach from Blackfriars Bridge, courtesy of Southwark Council

Right: Current view of South Bank from Waterloo Bridge
© Hayes Davidson
Below: Proposed view of South Bank from Waterloo Bridge
© Hayes Davidson

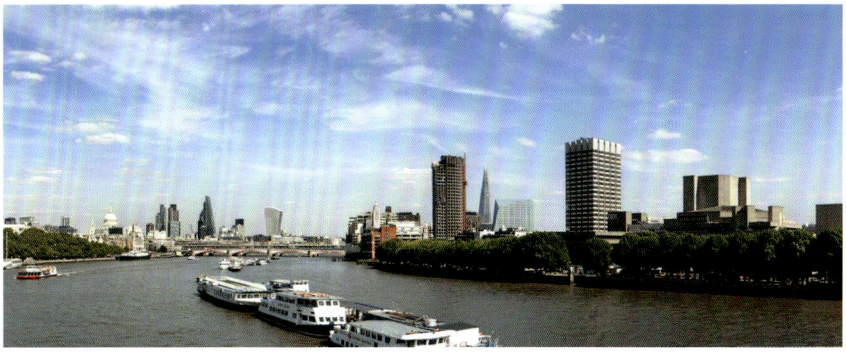

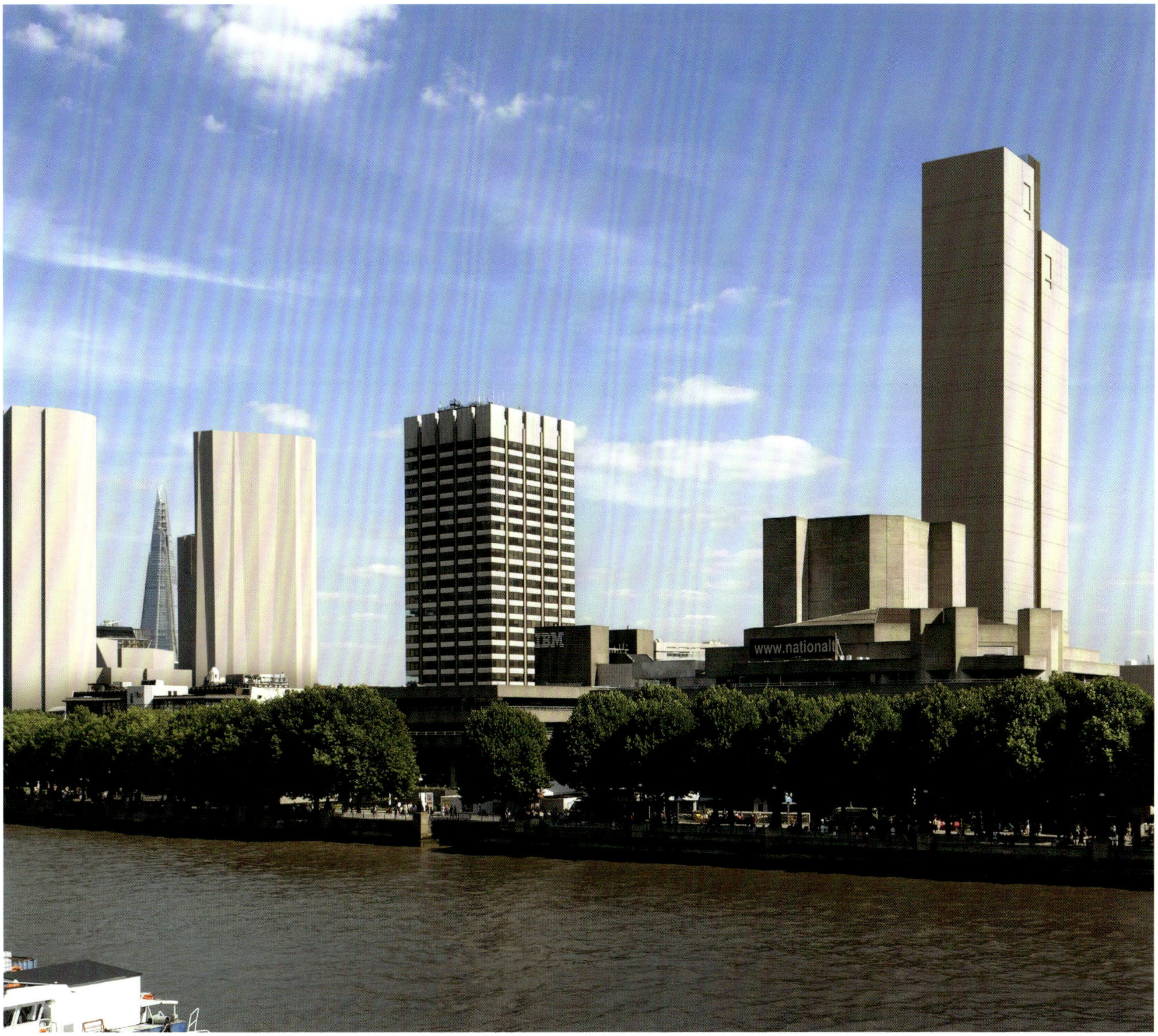
IBM
www.nationalt

Below: Shell Centre redevelopment by Squire + Partners for Canary Wharf Group and Qatari Diar, 2013 (proposed)

Right: Elizabeth House, by David Chipperfield Architects for Chelsfield and London & Regional Properties (proposed)

4.4 Waterloo

The London Plan identifies Waterloo as an Opportunity Area, which is expected to create 1,900 new homes by 2031 as well as much new large-scale office development around York Road and Waterloo Station.

Permission was granted in 2008 for a 144m tall residential tower on Doon Street, behind the National Theatre, after a public inquiry which followed objections by English Heritage and Westminster City Council about the lack of affordable housing and impacts on London views. Masterplanned by Lifschutz Davidson Sandilands, the Doon Street tower houses 329 flats with public uses at ground level. The surrounding development includes a new town square with lift and stairs to Waterloo Bridge and a leisure centre.

Two further nearby schemes have been the subject of controversy. Elizabeth House, a 1960s office block next to Waterloo Station, is to be redeveloped into a 29-storey office tower, designed by architect David Chipperfield for developer Chelsfield, with a double height gallery space at lower levels. While the project gained planning permission from Lambeth Council, a High Court judge ordered a judicial review of the DCLG's decision not to call in the scheme in late 2013, based on strong opposition from English Heritage and Westminster City Council due to its impact on the Palace of Westminster as a World Heritage site.

Plans to redevelop around 27-storey Shell Centre with an additional nine buildings containing nearly 900 homes, 900,000 sq ft commercial space, shops and restaurants, masterplanned by Squire & Partners, has also been the subject of a public enquiry, following a legal challenge mounted by Westminster City Council and other bodies.

Below: Proposals for Doon Street by Lifschutz Davidson Sandilands for Coin Street Community Builders

Below: Allies and Morrison's designs for Wood Wharf for Canary Wharf Group plc

Below: Wood Wharf masterplan, by Allies and Morrison for Canary Wharf Group plc, 2013

4.5 Canary Wharf & Wood Wharf

Canary Wharf Group are planning to extend their existing estate at Canary Wharf with a high density mixed-use development at Wood Wharf. The scheme comprises commercial, residential and hotel elements, grouped around a central square and surrounded on three sides by water, and will extend Canary Wharf's city-centre by nearly half. A masterplan by Allies and Morrison was submitted to Tower Hamlets Council in December 2013 for 3,100 homes, two million sq ft of commercial offices, and 250,000 sq ft of retail uses.

Responding to the recent shift in market demand, there is more residential emphasis and less on commercial space than the original masterplan outlined in 2009 by Rogers Stirk Harbour + Partners. The original 1,668 homes proposed are now doubled, while the five million sq ft of offices has been halved.

The first phase of the scheme includes five tall buildings, with two residential buildings designed by Stanton Williams, and two office buildings designed by Allies and Morrison. Swiss architects Herzog & de Meuron have also designed a 56-storey cylindrical residential skyscraper which features a signature 'stacking' style. Canary Wharf Group, which chose the practice for the tower, has said that 'it will set a new benchmark for high-rise residential design in London'.

The masterplan sets the taller residential towers around the perimeter, with the commercial offices at the centre, incorporating a range of floorplates to suit the needs of different businesses.

Below: Proposed public realm at Wood Wharf, with Herzog and de Meuron's One Wood Wharf in the background and A2/A3 by Stanton Williams on the right

Right: Current view of Isle of Dogs from Greenwich Park
© Hayes Davidson
Below: Proposed view of Isle of Dogs from Greenwich Park
© Hayes Davidson

88 LONDON'S GROWING UP!

89

4.6 Isle of Dogs & South Quay

The Isle of Dogs is designated as an Opportunity Area in the London Plan, with an indicative employment capacity of 110,000 and requirement for a minimum of 10,000 new homes by 2031. Tower Hamlets Council is keen to encourage new growth as a part of its efforts to regenerate and revitalise the community, but it is determined it should be 'the right growth.'

Marsh Wall, a road running through the centre of South Quay, is currently seeing proposals for a scale of development quite unprecedented in London, with 30 development sites between them looking to provide above the 10,000 new homes figure stated in the London Plan that could equate to the size of a new town. Situated in such close proximity, this is likely to result in a typology of tall towers much more similar to that of Vancouver or Hong Kong than has been seen in London before. Amongst these proposals is an 80-storey tower designed by Foster + Partners for the Berkeley Group, which includes 1.8 acres of public realm to open up the site; and a 75-storey (239m) tower designed by Squire and Partners for Chalegrove Properties, called 'City Pride'.

The towers' ability to increase the housing stock dramatically is attractive to the council. New affordable housing is a crucial element of Tower Hamlet's Local Plan: it aims to increase the provision of total housing by 3,000 homes each year for the next five years. The council's stated aspiration is that all commercial housing schemes should deliver affordable homes up to 50 per cent of the total development, subject to viability. Meeting this stipulation is a major factor in determining planning approval for new residential developments.

To ensure that the next phase of growth is managed properly, Tower Hamlets is drawing up a masterplan for the South Quay area, which will be supplementary to the Local Plan. The masterplan, which is being prepared by Tower Hamlets itself with the help of consultants, will be ready in 2014. Its brief is to 'deliver guidance for development that will help to shape the London skyline, deliver affordable housing and secure benefits for the local community resulting from development including the provision of new primary schools, open space and other community infrastructure'.

Tower Hamlets says its approach 'is intended to ensure that tall buildings are properly planned as part of an exercise in place-making informed by a clear long-term vision, rather than in an ad hoc, reactive piecemeal manner', warning that 'if these developments are not appropriately managed there is a risk that the townscape of Marsh Wall will suffer and development opportunities across the whole masterplan area will not be optimised resulting in a lost opportunity to deliver a sustainable place.'

Below: Arrowhead Quay, by Glenn Howells for Ballymore (proposed)

Below: City Pride by Squire and Partners for Chalegrove Properties Ltd (proposed)
Bottom: Western end of South West India Dock, with City Pride in foreground (proposed)

Below: Aldgate Place, by Allies and Morrison for Barratt London / British Land
Bottom: Goodman's Field, by Lifschutz Davidson Sandilands for Berkeley Homes.

Right: The Stage, Shoreditch by Pringle Brandon Perkins+Will for Plough Yard Developments Ltd

4.7 City Fringe

The GLA has defined three emerging tall building clusters within the City Fringe at Aldgate, Bishopsgate and Old Street, which could act as eastward extensions of the office in the City of London core and catalysts for regeneration.

In Aldgate, new developments include Goodman's Fields, a mixed use scheme ranging from 18 to 21 floors, with 920 new homes, student housing, hotel and ground floor uses currently under construction; and Aldgate Place, a development of three residential towers, hotel, office and retail uses. The City of London is also preparing a public realm strategy for the area to improve streets and public spaces.

Shoreditch is seeing significant change, particularly around Old Street, an area developing as a 'tech cluster' for London. There is a great deal of demand for residential schemes here, and proposals for tall buildings include: Principal Place, a mixed-use site including a residential tower designed by Foster + Partners; The Stage, a 40-storey residential tower designed by Pringle Brandon Perkins+Will which includes cultural uses; and Eagle House, an 82m tower for Mount Anvil designed by Farrells. The former Bishopsgate Goods Yard now known as The Goodsyard, is a 4.7 hectare site mixed-use scheme by Shoreditch High Street for which the masterplan went under consultation in late 2013. With a maximum of 350,000 sqm of development set for the site in an Interim Planning Guidance document and proposals for a large park, the proposed masterplan sets out that some areas will require very high densities, more typical of a central London area, and proposes a series of tall buildings to the west, decreasing towards the east to better fit the local context.

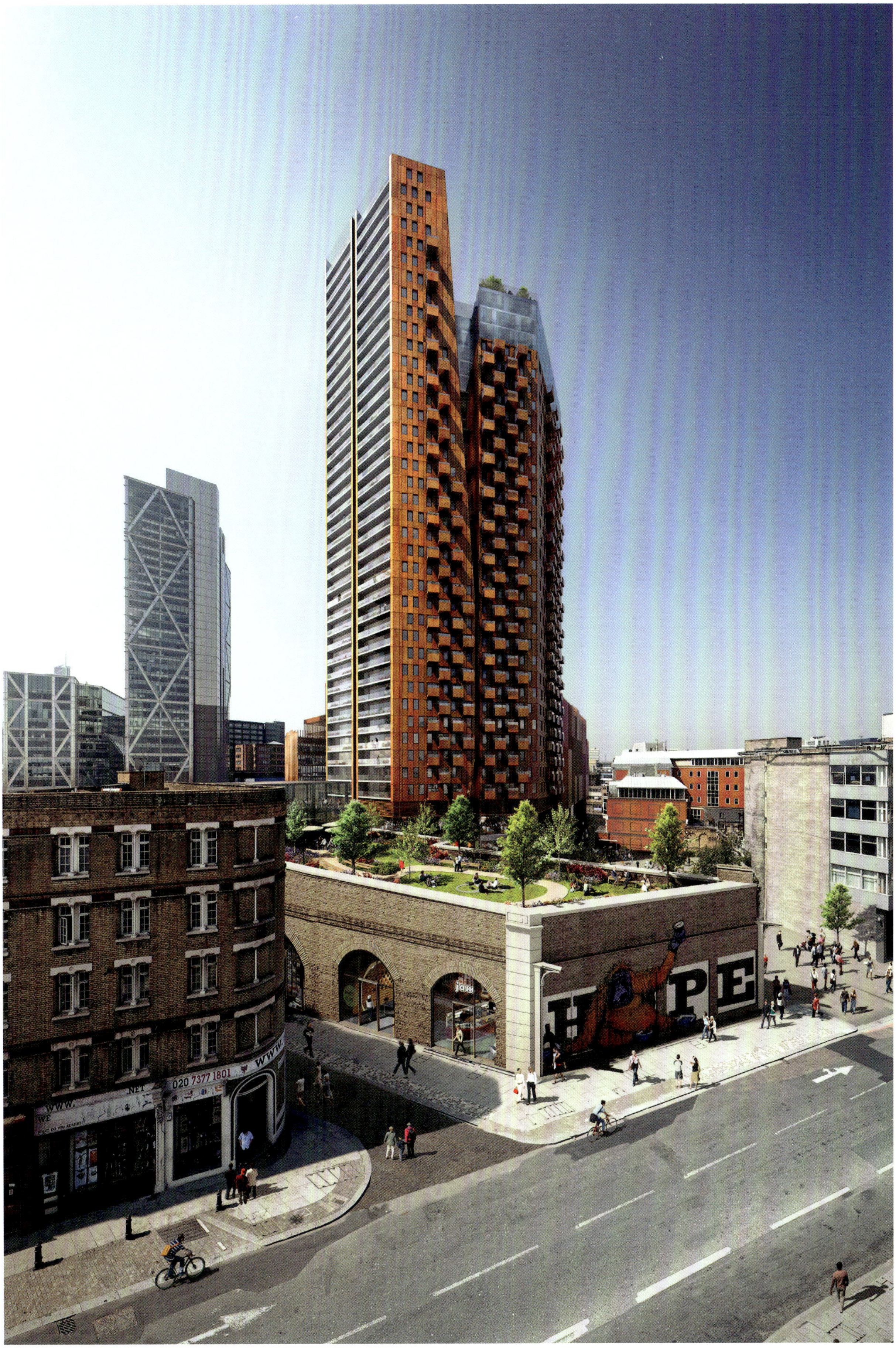
020 7377 1801

Below: Proposal for City Road Basin, by Bennetts Associates Architects, consented in 2005 with construction of the two towers now underway ©Assembly Studios

Bottom: Canaletto, City Road, by UN Studio/Axis Architects for Groveworld (proposed)

4.8 City Road Basin

The City Road Basin area sits between Angel and the Old Street roundabout on the Regent's Canal. A former industrial site, the area was largely inaccessible for some 100 years, but has been brought back into public use following a multi-million pound project to create public access to the waterway as part of a wider masterplan for City Road basin developed by developers Groveworld, British Waterways, Miller Development, Pembroke Real Estate, and masterplanners Bennetts Associates Architects.

The area has also started to become attractive to residential developers as the emergence of Old Street as a centre for technology and creative industries drives demand for high-quality residential properties in the surrounding area, and a number of high profile architects have been employed to work on high-rise residential developments.

The Canaletto tower is a 31-storey (100m) glass-and-steel tower designed by Dutch architects UNStudio, with three storeys of amenity space, including a spa and private cinema, below 190 apartments. Completion is due at the end of 2015. Across the road is Berkeley's City Forum, where Foster + Partners have designed a revised project for 250 City Road in Islington on behalf of Berkeley Homes. The plans include two towers of 42 and 36 storeys rising to heights of 155m and 137m. On another side of the canal basin at 261 Canal Road, is the 36-storey residential Lexicon Tower, designed by SOM, and currently under construction.

Below: Manhattan Loft Gardens, by SOM for Manhattan Loft Corporation (proposed)

Bottom: Aerial view of emerging buildings in Stratford, including the International Quarter, courtesy of Lend Lease

4.9 Stratford

Since the announcement that Stratford would host the 2012 Olympics in 2005, the area has seen a rise in interest from both domestic and international investors. The Olympic Park itself is now well underway with post-Games legacy planning, with a masterplan for 6,800 new homes across five new neighbourhoods in the 64-hectare site. Other developments planned include 'Olympicopolis', a project in the Olympic Park for the Victoria & Albert Museum and University College London to set up facilities there by 2018; the International Quarter, which will see 13 office and two residential buildings as well as a hotel; and iCity, a technology development where Loughborough University will establish a tech campus.

Elsewhere in Stratford, proposed schemes include the Stratford Plaza building by Telford Homes, a 26-storey, mixed use building next to Stratford bus and tube station, with 20 residential floors providing 260 flats; a Broadway Chambers development designed by Allies and Morrison with a 39-storey and a 20-storey building containing 388 apartments; Manhatttan Loft Gardens, designed by SOM for Manhattan Loft Corporation; and the 30- and 17-storey Glasshouse Gardens by Allies and Morrison, sited within the International Quarter for Lend Lease and London & Continental Railways.

Below: Proposals for Convoys Wharf, by Farrells for Hutchison Whampoa

Below: Royal Arsenal Riverside, by PRP Architects for Berkeley Homes (proposed)

4.10 Deptford, Lewisham and Greenwich

The London Plan identifies an Opportunity Area encompassing Deptford Creek/Greenwich Riverside and Lewisham/Catford/New Cross, with a minimum of 13,000 homes planned.

One of the most significant schemes in the area is the Hutchison Whampoa led scheme for 3,500 homes on Deptford's Convoys Wharf, in a £1bn regeneration project to transform a 40 acre wasteland which has been derelict for 13 years. Terry Farrell has created the masterplan for the area. The proposal has been under discussion with Lewisham Council but in October 2013 Mayor Boris Johnson decided to 'call in' the planning application, which means that the GLA, rather than Lewisham Council, will now determine whether or not planning permission is granted.

The Mayor said: 'We need to build thousands of new homes in the capital and proposals to do that at Convoys Wharf have been on the blocks for over a decade. Those plans deserve full and thorough consideration, and my team will work closely with the borough and the applicant to do so without further delay.'

The Mayor would not normally take over an application from a local authority until a decision had been made, but as London faces increasing pressure for new development, it is possible that the Mayor could use this power more regularly to speed up planning approvals.

In the past year at Greenwich Peninsula, a major regeneration area by the O2, outline planning permission has also been granted for 1,683 homes and two hotels, and detailed planning consent has been granted for the first phase of 506 homes, which are under construction. The homes are a combination of luxury private dwellings as well as affordable, including social and intermediate. The Peninsula Quays scheme, designed by Swanke Hayden Connell Architects, and given planning permission in 2013, includes residential towers of up to 32-storeys, with landscaped gardens, restaurants and stops.

And at Woolwich, further tall buildings are expected as developers look to maximise development potential when Crossrail comes to the area in 2019. The Royal Arsenal Riverside by developers Berkeley is a £1.5bn Thameside development that has been underway for the past five years and should be fully completed around 2030. The complex will embrace 5,000 homes, several hotels and cinemas, many shops and a variety of commercial work spaces.

Below: Greenwich Peninsula, courtesy of Pilbrow and Partners (proposed)

Below: No 1 Croydon (formerly the NLA tower), built 1970 by Richard Seifert & Partners, renovated in 2008 by AHMM

Top: One Landsowne Road, by CZWG Architects for Guildhouse-Rosepride (proposed)
Middle: Morello Tower, by Make Architects for Menta (proposed)
Bottom: Proposal for redevelopment of Nestlé Tower to residential apartments, by EPR Architects for Legal & General

4.11 Croydon

Croydon is one of the few outer London boroughs with a number of existing tall office buildings, mostly built in the 1960s and 1970s. More recently, there has been another major redevelopment programme for Croydon town centre, which has seen several new tall buildings proposed, including Morello London, a 55-storey residential tower clad in bronze anodized aluminum, designed by Make as part of a mixed-use development along Cherry Orchard Road; and One Landsdowne Road, a 55-storey tower designed by CZWG, accommodating a hotel, private and serviced apartments, new leisure centre, restaurant and cantilevered viewing gallery.

The tallest tower to date opened in March 2014 – Saffron Square, a 134m, 44-storey residential tower with 414 apartments, designed by Rolfe Judd Architects. As the area sees more demand for homes, plans are afoot to convert the Nestlé Tower into 288 residential apartments, designed by EPR.

Below: Imperial West by PLP and Aukett Fitzroy Robinson for Imperial College London (proposed)

Below: White City OAPF masterplan, courtesy of GLA

4.13 White City and Earls Court

The White City Opportunity Area covers approximately 272 acres on the eastern edge of the London Borough of Hammersmith & Fulham, along the boundary with the Royal Borough of Kensington & Chelsea. Up to 5,000 homes and 10,000 jobs are planned for the area. One of the key objectives is to encourage offices, hotels and flexible work spaces and to 'offer creative, media, bio-medical research and development industries that build on the presence of the BBC, Imperial College London, Westfield and Hammersmith Hospital.'

An OAPF for the area gives general guidance on building heights and locations for tall buildings, noting that the majority of new buildings should be medium rise of six to ten storeys with some lower-rise three to six storey terraces. However, some 'slender' towers of approximately 21-31 storeys could be appropriate on certain sites such as the Westway.

One of the major developments is at Imperial West, a new campus for Imperial College, which includes a 35-storey tapering residential tower designed by architects PLP, masterplanned by Aukett Fitzroy Robinson. Other local plans include the next phase of Westfield, which includes a 20-storey tower.

Plans for the 77-acre £8 billion redevelopment in Earls Court and West Kensington to create 7,500 new homes also includes a 'cluster' of tall buildings around the existing Empress State Building within a largely low-mid rise masterplan for 7,500 homes and thousands of permanent jobs.

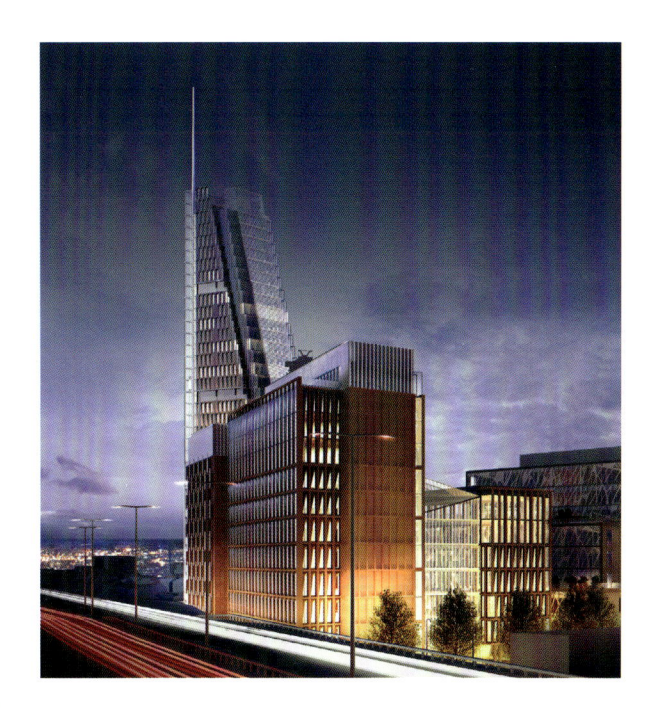

Below: Masterplan for Brent Cross Cricklewood, by Allies and Morrison for Hammerson, 2014

3.13 Brent Cross Cricklewood

Brent Cross Cricklewood is a 55 hectare site in north London, just off the M1, which has been earmarked for a £4 billion investment programme, and is an Opportunity Area in the London Plan. Led by Hammerson and Standard Life Investments as BXC Development Partners, the scheme includes plans for 7,500 homes, new offices, four parks, transport improvements (including £200 million on road improvements, expanded bus station and a new train station), a new health centre, schools and an extension of the Brent Cross Shopping Centre.

Architects Allies and Morrison have drawn up a masterplan for the scheme, which includes new green spaces, bridges over the North Circular Road and a green boulevard leading into Brent Cross Main Square. The scheme includes permission for a number of tall buildings, which are 'clustered…as landmarks on the skyline, interspersed with smaller scale buildings and generous open spaces.'

In 2010, Barnet Council commissioned a Tall Buildings study for the whole borough, defining the predominant character of Barnet as two to three storeys, and 'tall buildings' as those over eight storeys. It suggests that over the next 15 years it expects more pressure for tall buildings, which will offer the opportunity for more intensive use but should not detract from the nature of the surrounding area:

'The proposals for the Brent Cross/Cricklewood area anticipate a significant rise in scale from the existing context, particularly in the area to the south of the north circular and east of the railway mainline. Existing plans show scope for a significant cluster of tall buildings up to 25 storeys tall in the area and particularly notes the inclusion of a tall building at the southern end of the M1 which will have a role as a citywide landmark.'

The masterplan for the scheme was given planning approval by the Mayor and Barnet Council in 2010, and the first phase of the scheme is due to start on site next year. This centres on Brent Cross shopping centre and will be refurbished with new shops, hotels, restaurants and leisure facilities, accommodated on the land of the current car park. It will also include new bridges over the North Circular Road, the new expanded bus station, improvements to the River Brent, key junctions, landscaping and around 1,250 homes. The rest of the development will come forward over the next 25 years in six phases.

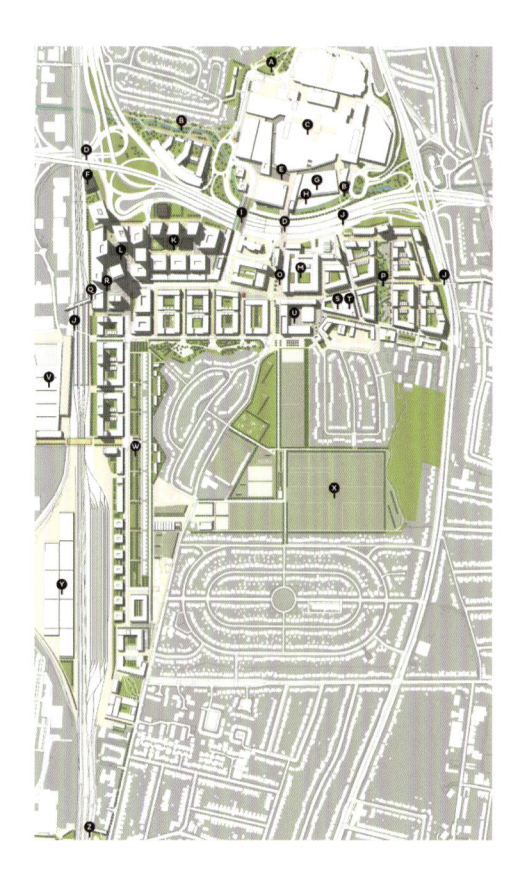

Masterplan — Brent Cross Cricklewood

A   Sturgess Park
B   River Brent and new Brent Riverside Park
C   Brent Cross Shopping Centre
D   New pedestrian and cycle bridge
E   New Brent Cross Main Square
F   Combined Heat and Power Plant
G   Multiplex cinema and leisure facilities
H   Bigger Brent Cross bus station
I   New Templehof Bridge
J   Pedestrian bridge
K   New office district square
L   New office district
M   New food store
N   Brent Cross Tube Station
O   New Market Square
P   New Eastern Park
Q   New railway station
R   New Station Square
S   New community facilities and health centre
T   New leisure centre
U   New Whitefield School
V   New wast and recycling facility
W   New Brent Terrace Park
X   Clitterhouse Playing Fields
Y   Rail freight facility
Z   Cricklewood Station

Below: Proposals for Old Oak Common, courtesy of GLA

4.14 Old Oak Common

Old Oak Common, an industrial site located between Harlesden and Acton between the boroughs of Hammersmith and Fulham, Brent and Ealing, is poised for major redevelopment thanks to the development of a new Crossrail station, providing a direct interchange between the proposed HS2 route by 2026.

The GLA, together with local authorities, are seeking to develop a 30-year vision for the area, which they believe has capacity for up to 90,000 jobs and 19,000 new homes, schools, open spaces, shops and leisure facilities. Based on the concept of encouraging high-density development around transport nodes, the London Plan suggests that this area could support a cluster of tall buildings around the interchange.

Stadium Capital Developments, who also have proposals to develop a 40,000 capacity football stadium for Queens Park Rangers on the site have said: 'We envisage a new vibrant, mixed-use and high-quality entertainment and leisure development, which will turn this neglected but tremendously well-connected area into a new world-class city quarter.

'We are talking to a number of world-class architects to design iconic tall buildings akin to New York, the Far East and London's finest, as well as improving and incorporating the waterside environment of the Grand Union Canal. We have assembled a top-class professional team to design tens of thousands of new homes, a 350 bedroom luxury hotel and millions of square feet of entertainment and leisure focused commercial space including: retail, studios and offices, bars and clubs, restaurants, cinemas and other leisure accommodation.'

Although Old Oak Common hasn't yet seen any applications for tall buildings, it represents one in the next wave of as yet untapped regeneration areas for London, most of which require significant new transport infrastructure to unlock their development potential. As London's existing opportunity areas are built out, the arrival of major new transport infrastructure such as HS2, and Crossrail 2 and 3 are likely to drive the development of new areas of high-density high-rise development in London.

CHAPTER 5
London's future skyline

The opprobrium heaped on tall buildings in the 70s and 80s as a result of grim high-rise local authority housing estates – 'concrete monstrosities' – has dissipated in recent years with the emergence of a more elegant strain of skyscraper. 30 St Mary Axe designed by Foster + Partners brought a new distinction to the design of tall buildings in London. Its bullet shape and spiral decoration soon became a new icon for the capital, reflecting an image of modernity and style. Likewise, the simple form and elegant proportions of The Shard by Renzo Piano has proved highly popular with the public and media and shouts 'London' to the world.

The improving popularity of tall buildings is reflected in the poll conducted by NLA and Ipsos Mori into Londoners' views on tall towers where 40 per cent of respondents did not agree with the statement that 'there are too many tall buildings in London' compared to 34 per cent who agreed. 46 per cent agreed that tall buildings have made London look better, while only 25 per cent disagreed.

53 per cent of people thought that how a building looks in its surroundings was the most important consideration when deciding whether a new tall building should be allowed to get built. This was followed by good design and the provision of affordable homes. How tall it was came last on the list with just 11 per cent.

These figures disguise a more complex picture when analysed at a local level. When Soundings, specialists in public consultation tried to find out what people in the area thought about tall buildings proposed for the Bishopsgate Goodyard there was little unanimity. People in Shoreditch 'tech-city' suggested that they could 'live with height' but only if the buildings were of a 'very high quality'. Those living in Banglatown around Brick Lane saw the height as aspirational, and were excited. Local businesses and traders there thought, for the greater part, that the tall buildings will signal a positive shift.

Those opposed tended to be the middle class settlers and artist communities – exemplified by the East End Preservation Society fronted by broadcaster Dan Cruickshank – who see the development of their part of the city as a destructive act.

At a wider level there are critics of policy and intent. Simon Jenkins, journalist and chairman of the National Trust, has said: 'The London skyline is an almighty car crash. We have a real planning issue. The pass has been sold in the past 20-30 years. A policy existed but it crumbled… The policy now is to have no policy.'

Alan Liebowitz, of the developer Dorrington has observed that the wave of tall buildings sweeping the capital is driven by 'vanity and ego. There is a competitive urge to build bigger, build taller and in a different shape to shout "Here I am." It astounds me that we are prepared to allow tall buildings to randomly exaggerate, plunder and privatise our precious skyline.' Liebowitz's main contention is that there is no vision for London – 'no comprehensive approach, no realization of cumulative effect.'

But is it just ego and vanity driving the growth of tall building? London will become the first city in Europe to be home to 10 million people by 2030; this means half a million new jobs and a million more people to be housed. At the same time there are planning policies that support the densification of the Greater London area as opposed to a return of post war policies of developing green field sites around the south east region (although many believe this will become necessary in the future).

According to Sir Edward Lister, deputy mayor for planning, in the light of these pressures of growth 'what we can't do is impose some kind of freeze on the skyline and suspend the capital in stasis.'

He believes the Opportunity Area Planning Frameworks and Local Plans provide clear enough guidance for boroughs and developers about the right places in which to locate tall buildings and how they should be built. 'London has struck the right balance between too much prescription and too little control.'

Most commentators would agree that in the right place, tall buildings can make positive contributions to city life as stated in the joint report published in 2007 English Heritage and CABE. The report reinforced the importance of the quality of tall buildings at ground level. How they touch the ground and impact on the surrounding area are key. Tall buildings can release land to provide new public space, an example of which can be seen in the linking of the ground plane below the Eastern Cluster in the City of London. Here there is an integrated strategy that includes the space below the Pinnacle, the public atrium at the base of The Leadenhall Building and the existing public squares outside the Aviva Tower and 30 St Mary Axe as well as a series of other new towers in the area. Urban design guidelines should deliver good public space, assist urban integration and control environmental factors such as sun, shade and microclimate.

The English Heritage/CABE report included the caveat that if towers are too big and too prominent, such buildings can harm the qualities that people value about a place; and there are increasing pressures for buildings to be big and prominent.

The pressures are from London's unprecedented growth, from international investors and purchasers for whom tall residential buildings are the norm, from boroughs' dependence on Section 106 agreements with developers that pay for affordable housing and local improvements, from values that increase as you go higher and from the attraction to well-heeled occupiers of spectacular views across the capital. These are pressures the planning system has not had to deal with heretofore and so we suggest that we need to beef up the level of control, while maintaining the approach to planning which is a key part of London's DNA.

Since the Great Fire, London's planning policies have generally been driven by a sense of pragmatism rather than grand visions, frequently in response to commercial pressures and economic circumstance. In contrast, other established cities, according to a report prepared by LSE Cities, notably Paris and New York, are the results of logical 'top-down' planning and co-ordinated development.

In Paris, the tall buildings policy defines three distinct building height zones. In the old centre, buildings cannot exceed six storeys in height. On the fringe, tall buildings are permitted provided they adhere to a set of specified guidelines, while in the Zone d'Action Concert (ZAC), where La Défense commercial centre is located, there are no height restrictions.

New York City has historically attempted to control the configuration and siting of tall buildings through a range of tight zoning mechanisms. Despite these the city is facing similar pressures to London; luxury housing development is booming. Developers are catering to the global elite and ultra-rich who will pay premium prices for apartments with spectacular views. A recent report – *The Accidental Skyline* – by the Municipal Arts Society highlights the rise of super tall, super slim towers including 432 Park Avenue and 217 West 57th Street which will dwarf the Empire State and Chrysler Buildings.

Vancouver has developed a very specific plan which allows low- to mid-rise mixed-use developments to define the urban street pattern and a series of spaced out towers to create the required density. This planning policy, which has become known as 'Vancouverism', also allows for generous parks and accessibility to the city's waterside amenities to create a very liveable city.

The LSE report suggested that London needed more positive planning for tall building in specific areas, in contrast to the negative approach exemplified by the protected view corridor system which dictates where tall building cannot, rather than where they can, be built. The report pointed out that Canary Wharf and similar Dockland regeneration programmes have already established a model: well-designed, densely populated complexes – including a number of tall buildings – that are easily accessible by public transport. The volumes of the buildings of the first phase of Canary Wharf were designed some 25 years ago by masterplanners SOM, and the completed towers have followed precisely the form of that original masterplan in a way that just does not happen elsewhere in the capital.

The GLA has responded to the LSE report with the planning frameworks for the development of opportunity areas around the capital – like Vauxhall Nine Elms, Croydon, Stratford and Old Oak Common – places designated for tall building clusters where local community reaction to tall building is less of an issue, indeed where it is seen as positive economic benefit.

But one must question whether the systems we have in place are robust enough in the face of the pressures

Right: La Défense in Paris, with low-rise buildings in the foreground
Below: Proposed new residential towers in New York from The Accidental Skyline, courtesy of Municipal Arts Society
Bottom: The skyline of Vancouver. Photography: Peter Murray

432 Park Ave.	53 West 53rd St.	157 West 57th St.	220 Central Park South
1396′	1050′	1004′	920′
	111 West 57th St.	217 West 57th St.	
	1350′	Up to 1550′	

to develop when one looks at the form of the emerging cluster at Vauxhall Nine Elms. This was defined in 2012 as a 'series of tall buildings coming forward as separate individual elements on the skyline to a maximum of 150 metres with the pinnacle being formed by the Vauxhall Tower at 180 metres.' Today it would seem that the pinnacle of the cluster will more likely be One Nine Elms at height closer to 200m. Not that there is necessarily anything wrong with a 200m tower in this location, but it suggests a worryingly flexible approach to the creation of a key new piece of city. We need firmer plans for these areas, plans that are stuck to.

On the other hand we should beware that the wide area controls of Paris has delivered a rational but essentially sterile city centre. London's pragmatic approach to planning is part of its DNA; the gallimaufry of styles, the contrast and clashes are part of the excitement and character of the capital. It is a characteristic the City of London has succeeded in retaining as it has grown increasingly tall.

Neither does New York provide the right answer, its as-of-right-system delivering a regularity of form and detail that would not sit well in London's less orthogonal layout.

Nevertheless we have to accept that – like New York – we are facing unprecedented pressures to build taller and taller; one must ask the question whether we have the will or the powers to ensure that the quality and scale of new development is commensurate with the impact they will have on the character of the city and the experience of Londoners.

We can all agree that tall buildings should be of the highest architectural quality and designed in full cognisance of their likely impact on the immediate surroundings and the wider environment. To ensure that happens, while delivering essential economic growth and many thousands of homes, the Mayor needs to beef up his design advice. He should set up a London Skyline Commission – a group who can look at the totality of tall building development in London and assess the impact that it is having on the shape of the city. To support the Commission the Mayor should make greater use of 3D computer visualisations that are available to him and would allow new proposals to be seen in the wider context. This digital model would be a valuable tool for public consultation.

The Commission would provide design review, taking into account the historic context as well as the new buildings emerging in the vicinity. It should provide advice throughout the process from the selection of architects through to the detailed construction of the building and help to ensure that as London goes through this period of unprecedented growth and physical change, in a period when local authority resources are stretched, we do not make the mistakes of the 60s and litter the capital's skyline with disparate monstrosities that will blight London for generations to come.

Collected comments

"What we can't do is impose some kind of freeze on the skyline and suspend the capital in stasis."
Sir Edward Lister, Deputy Mayor for Policy and Planning

"Dramatic changes to the London skyline are happening fast and with little debate beyond individual borough boundaries. This is not about stifling change, but recognising that there are alternatives which deliver economic growth without robbing London of the distinctiveness which is key to its success."
Rosemarie MacQueen, Strategic Director Built Environment, City of Westminster

"The fact that London needs new homes is a poor excuse for short-sighted policymaking on the hoof."
Alan Leibowitz, Joint Managing Director, Dorrington

"There has been a shift from the occasional tall building to tall buildings becoming a panacea for solving problems of density, housing and green space."
Nigel Barker, Planning and Conservation Director for London, English Heritage

"The opportunity to build tall brings with it the possibility to create grand, 21st century public spaces. The taller the building, the greater our responsibility to provide an appropriate public gesture to the city at ground level."
Graham Stirk, Partner, Rogers Stirk Harbour + Partners

"There's a general presumption against tall buildings in this city but it's a position that's at odds with the innovative, energetic spirit that is London."
Amanda Levete, Director, AL_A

"Really tall buildings need really good architects – not least to create really friendly ground planes."
Paul Finch, Chair, Design Council Cabe

"Our continued survival on this planet, in the face of a million inhabitants urbanizing every week, relies on densifying our cities."
Antony Wood, Executive Director, Council on Tall Buildings and Urban Habitat

"The unique character of London has always been its ability to embrace change without ignoring its history or culture."
Michael Squire, Senior Partner, Squire and Partners

"We must not fall into the post-war trap of allowing poorly designed buildings to sprout up. To do so would risk damaging not only London's economy, but its heritage and aesthetic qualities for decades to come."
Alexander Jan, Director, Arup

"Hong Kong, one of the most dense cities in the world uses 16 times less, transport related, energy per capita compared to most North American cities. Dense cities with high rise buildings can be more sustainable than low rise low density cities."
Gerard Maccreanor, Director, Maccreanor Lavington

"How will [tall buildings] cope with our changing needs, the requirements of an ageing population, future environmental and technological issues? Towers ought to be designed with loose fit principles in mind to have the longest possible useful lifespan."
Alex Lifschutz, Director, Lifschutz Davidson Sandilands

"Over the next ten years I predict that we will see more of an emphasis on quality of materials, detail and proportion rather the need to make every building a landmark."
Paul Monaghan, Director, Allford Hall Monaghan Morris

REFERENCES

REFERENCES

Chapter one

Vision 2020 (2013)
By Mayor of London

Urban Task Force, Towards an Urban Renaissance (1999)
By Lord Rogers

Tall Buildings Report (2002)
By the Transport, Local Government and Regions Committee, House of Commons

Create Streets: Not just multi-storey estates (2013)
By Create Streets

Tall Towers 2012 – London's High-Rise Residential Developments (2012)
By Knight Frank

The Towers of London (2012)
By Savills

Office vs. Residential: the Economics of Building Tall (2013)
By James Barton and Steve Watts, Davis Langdon (AECOM)

Revised Early Minor Alterations to the London Plan (2013)
By Greater London Authority

Draft Further Alterations to the London Plan (2014)
By Greater London Authority

London View Management Framework supplementary planning guidance (2012)
By Greater London Authority

City of London Core Strategy (2011)
By City of London Corporation

Tall Buildings Evidence Paper (2010)
By the City of London Corporation

Revitalise – a Borough-wide Tall Building Research Paper (2010)
By Southwark Council

Elephant and Castle Opportunity Area Supplementary Planning Document (SPD) (2012)
By Southwark Council and GLA

Guidance on Tall Buildings (2007)
By Commission for Architecture and the Built Environment (CABE) and English Heritage

Planning Policy Guidance 1 – Design (1997)
By the Department of the Environment

Chapter two

London High – a guide to the past, present and future of London's skyscrapers (2006)
By Herbert Wright

Towards the London Plan (2001)
By Greater London Authority

Interim strategic planning guidance on tall buildings, strategic views and the skyline in London (2001)
By Greater London Authority

Chapter four

Vauxhall Nine Elms Battersea Opportunity Area Planning Framework (2012)
By GLA, Lambeth Council, Wandsworth Council, TfL, English Heritage

Core Strategy – Development Plan Document (2010)
By Wandsworth Council

Blackfriars Road SPD (2014)
By Southwark Council

Southbank: London's Transforming Skyline (2013)
By CBRE

Core Strategy 2025 – Development Plan Document (2010)
By Tower Hamlets

White City Opportunity Area Planning Framework (2013)
By GLA, Hammersmith and Fulham Council, TfL

Tall Buildings Study of London Borough of Barnet (2010)
By Barnet Council

Old Oak – a Vision for the Future (2013)
By Transport for London, Hammersmith & Fulham Council, Brent Council, Ealing Council and the Mayor of London

Chapter five

The Accidental Skyline (2013)
By the Municipal Arts Society

Tall Buildings: vision of the future or victims of the past (2002)
By LSE for Development Securities PLC

Other general sources

New City – contemporary architecture in the City of London (2013)
By Alec Forshaw

Tall building policy making and implementation in central London: visual impacts on regionally protected views from 2000 to 2008 (2011)
By Juergen Kufner

Building Tall in a 2,000-year-old City (2013)
By Peter Murray

The Council on Tall Buildings and Urban Habitat – various references

---

With special thanks to: Nigel Barker – English Heritage; Thomas Bender – Design Council Cabe; Nigel Bidwell – Farrells; Peter Bishop; Peter Farnham – Tower Hamlets Council; Paul Katz – KPF; Simon Lay – AECOM; Robin Meakins – Barton Willmore; Peter Rees – City of London Corporation; Jane Richards – WSP Group; Paul Runaghan – Farrells; Brian Smith – AECOM; Ken Shuttleworth – Make; Dan Taylor – Southwark Council; Colin Wilson – GLA

PROFILES

PROFILES

Sponsors:

GL Hearn

GL Hearn is one of the UK's leading independent property consultancies providing trusted commercial property advice to the public sector, developers, investors and occupiers. Our goal is a simple one – to understand our clients' business, bring our expertise and enthusiasm to bear and work with them to create, develop, protect and enhance their business interests.

Our strategy informs our approach to any given project and we are fortunate at GL Hearn to be one of the country's top 20 multi-disciplinary consultancies with highly experienced specialists in valuation, investment, planning and building consultancy. Our clients place their trust in us for actionable advice and it is this aspect of our service that has kept us thriving as a business from our modest beginnings in 1923 to the successful national organisation we have become today.

280 High Holborn,
London WC1V 7EE
0207 851 4900
info@glhearn.com
www.glhearn.com

IAN SIMPSON ARCHITECTS

Since the practice was founded by Rachel Haugh and Ian Simpson in 1987, it has compiled an impressive portfolio of award-winning projects. Its initiation was motivated by a shared belief in the power of high quality design to lead the regeneration of post-industrial cities and instigate new contemporary architectural identities. As projects have increased in scale over the years, these original values have matured and been reinforced such that they remain the practice's guiding principles.

The underlying themes of urban renewal, sustainability and design excellence unite an otherwise diverse range of building functions and solutions. Similarly, the completed work demonstrates that the practice's regeneration objectives are equally valid whether applied to new buildings or to existing historic structures. Its innovative solutions for cultural venues, transport interchanges, schools, colleges and high density living have both challenged normative design responses and contributed positive new precedents.

5-8 Roberts Place,
London EC1R 0BB
020 7549 4000
info@iansimpsonarchitects.com
www.iansimpsonarchitects.com

JLL

As a global financial and professional services firm specialising in real estate, JLL provides integrated services delivered by expert teams worldwide to clients seeking increased value by owning or investing in real estate. Our 2,400 employees in the UK offer every aspect of commercial and residential property service from development consulting and financing through to agency leasing and investment, as well as every type of management, professional advisory and sustainability service. Across the globe JLL is at the heart of cities and nowhere is this more evident than London where we have been involved with some of the capital's most iconic tall buildings, from Canary Wharf to The Shard and The Leadenhall Building. We understand the unique approach required for this type of product and combine our global capacity and best practice with our on the ground knowledge and expertise to deliver results that ensure our client's vision becomes reality.

30 Warwick Street,
London W1B 5NH
020 7493 4933
www.jll.co.uk

M3 CONSULTING

Since 1997, M3 Consulting has worked alongside public and private sector clients as independent consultants and development managers to add value to their properties in all stages of the development lifecycle. We are a team of property, design and construction professionals who solve property challenges and deliver successful projects with energy, expertise and commitment. With flexible services tailored to each client and project, we have completed projects ranging from £50,000 to £2bn in value. Our portfolio spans across commercial, residential, arts / education, community, leisure, transport and mixed-use schemes. In the last year alone, our hands-on, innovation-focused approach to management and problem solving has ushered a number of notable successes, including achieving practical completion of NEQ mixed-use quarter at Regent's Place, topping out of the 50-storey The Leadenhall Building, and planning for the 105,000 sqm Sampson House and Ludgate House development.

Dashwood House,
69 Old Broad Street,
London EC2M 1QS
020 7710 4400
www.m3c.co.uk

MONTAGU EVANS

Montagu Evans LLP is a practice of Chartered Surveyors. Our Town Planning Department, led by ten partners, is widely recognised for its experience and expertise in securing permissions. Montagu Evans expertise in negotiation stems from being involved at the outset of projects when the site is being bought – advising on what sites are suitable and deliverable from a political as well as a planning perspective.

In addition to securing permissions our advice includes: confidential site appraisals and reviews of existing consents; advising on the brief for the site; appearing at EiP's and appeal inquiries; Townscape and Heritage Assessments, working as part of development teams to promote development in sensitive locations; and viability analysis and affordable housing, providing expertise in negotiations on the provision of affordable housing.

We are advising on proposals for tall buildings in: Camden, City of London, Hackney, Hammersmith & Fulham, Islington, Lambeth, Newham, Southwark and Wandsworth.

5 Bolton Street,
London W1J 8BA
020 7493 4002
www.montagu-evans.co.uk

Turner & Townsend

Turner & Townsend is a leading global programme management and construction consultancy that supports organisations that invest in, own and operate assets. Working from 80 offices in 33 countries, we are making the difference to projects across the property, infrastructure and natural resources sectors worldwide. We help organisations succeed by managing risk while maximising value and performance during the construction and operation of their assets. Having project managed The Shard at London Bridge Quarter, we continue to work on tall buildings and large-scale developer projects across the globe.

7 Savoy Court,
Strand,
London WC2R 0EX
020 7544 4000
www.turnerandtownsend.com
@turntown

Supporters:

British Land

British Land is a real estate investment company based in London and listed on the London Stock Exchange. We create value by actively managing, financing and developing prime commercial property to provide the environment in which modern business can thrive. British Land owns or manages real estate worth £17.1 billion (British Land share £11.2 billion), with Central London offices comprising 40% of the portfolio. Sustainability is at the core of the business – from community involvement in the planning process, through development, refurbishment and management, the aim is to provide attractive buildings that minimise resource use and meets the needs of occupiers today and tomorrow.

CANARY WHARF LONDON

Canary Wharf is a major new central business district in London. No other business district in a major European city offers occupiers the flexibility of design from a developer with an unsurpassed track record of delivering buildings. The district comprises circa 17 million sq ft of office and retail space with a working population of approximately 100,000 people. With retail of 848,000 sq ft including 280 of the best shops, bars and restaurants, health clubs and other amenities, 30 acres of intricately landscaped public spaces, an extensive year round arts and events programme, Canary Wharf allows office occupiers an unrivalled working lifestyle.

EuropeanLand

European Land is a developer and development manager currently focused on the mixed-use Merchant Square scheme at Paddington Basin. The scheme comprises 6 buildings constructed around a new canalside garden square: Merchant Square. This will include the iconic 1 Merchant Square; at 42 floors it will be the tallest building in Westminster when finished. European Land has an excellent development track record, with highlights including The Point and Waterside Buildings, Paddington Walk and Kings Chelsea.

York House,
45 Seymour Street,
London W1H 7LX
020 7486 4466
www.britishland.com

One Canada Square,
London E14 5AB
020 7418 2000
www.canarywharf.com

The Waterline,
31 Harbet Road,
Paddington,
London W2 1JS
020 7298 0800
www.merchantsquare.co.uk

PROFILES

Associate Sponsors:

TIAA Henderson Real Estate

TIAA Henderson Real Estate (TH Real Estate) is a major investor in the global property market with offices across Asia and Europe, managing c.$23bn of real estate assets, across c.50 funds and mandates. Our alliance with TIAA-CREF in North America increases our global AUM to c.$71bn.

Born from two successful organisations, TIAA-CREF and Henderson Global Investors, we have a combined track record of over 90 years in global real estate.

Our products are managed by specialist teams, which are supported by our senior management and an integrated investment platform, including finance, debt and currency management, performance analytics, client service, fund and transaction structuring, development, sustainability and research.

We manage pooled funds and segregated accounts for both individual and club-based investors to invest in properties offering core and value-add returns. As well as investing across all commercial sectors, we specialise in five key franchises: retail, offices, logistics, commercial real estate debt and multi-family.

201 Bishopsgate
London
EC2M 3BN
020 3727 8000
contact@threalestate.com
www.threalestate.com

AECOM

London is big, bustling and beautiful. It's a complex place and we love it. But how do you keep the capital moving and make roads safer; build up sustainably; keep parks part of the story? Our expert planners, designers, engineers and project managers understand London and work to keep it great. In response to growing demands and greater unpredictability, they use 360 ingenuity to provide smart solutions, helping our clients and London's communities to see further and go further.

Environmental, social and economic sustainability is at the heart of everything we do. From saving icons like the BBC's Broadcasting House to providing the vision behind the Olympic Park; from massive infrastructure projects like Crossrail to updating London's water networks; from project managing western Europe's tallest, The Shard, to renovating the Houses of Parliament, our teams are focused on making London an even better place to live, work and visit.

MidCity Place,
71 High Holborn,
London WC1V 6QS
020 7645 2000
www.aecom.com

ARUP

Arup is a global leader in the engineering of tall buildings and has been one of the most significant players in the evolution of London's skyline. Our expertise played a crucial role in the design of ground breaking buildings of the 1980s, such as the Lloyds Building, and, later, the Swiss Re building and Heron Tower and, more recently towers such as the Shard and 122 Leadenhall Street.

We are currently at work on a number of tall buildings planned for the City of London, east London and along the south bank of the Thames. Arup's vision for the future of tall buildings focuses on better design, engineering solutions that allow for more rapid construction, and lowering the total cost of high rise projects.

Arup is an employee-owned firm of engineers, designers, planners, consultants and technical specialists. We bring creativity and technical excellence to everything we do.

13 Fitzroy Street,
London W1T 4BQ
020 7636 1531
www.arup.com

Nullifire

Nullifire are world leaders in the provision of intumescent coatings and passive fire protection solutions. Our products protect property, minimise business losses, and safeguard lives. That's why there are no compromises with Nullifire. We are a true specialist focused solely on fire protection, and dedicated to innovation.

We work with many of the world's leading architects and contractors, providing fire protection solutions for iconic structures across the globe. The company enjoys an industry-wide reputation for both its expertise and its holistic approach to protecting a building. Nullifire's range offers trusted solutions to protect steel structures, service penetrations and construction movement joints. Recently Nullifire have launched SC902, a new generation hybrid coating capable of protecting steel work for up to 120 minutes in one application, saving up to 60% on the installation time. Ideal for tall buildings requiring a high fire rating, SC902 is revolutionising passive fire protection.

Torrington Avenue,
Coventry CV4 9TJ
024 7685 5000
protect@nullifire.com
www.nullifire.com

RIBA Architecture.com

RIBA champions better buildings, communities and the environment through architecture and our members. We provide the standards, training, support and recognition that put our members – in the UK and overseas – at the peak of their profession. With government, we work to improve the design quality of public buildings, new homes and new communities. Our collection of architectural drawings, photographs and archives is one of the largest and most important in the world, and we stage exhibitions, talks, events and awards (including the prestigious RIBA Stirling Prize) that help people see their surroundings in a completely new way.

66 Portland Place,
London W1 1AD
020 7580 5533
info@riba.org
www.architecture.com
@RIBA

savills

Savills is one of the world's largest real estate firms, with a rich heritage for providing premium residential and commercial property services of the highest calibre. Established in 1855, we have 25,000 employees and over 500 offices throughout the Americas, Europe, Asia Pacific, Africa and the Middle East, with a turnover of £806.4m. Savills is the leading UK property advisory firm, voted as UK Business Superbrand for the 6th consecutive year in 2014. Our coverage of the UK is unrivalled with over 95 offices, encompassing over 150 service lines and over 3,200 staff, with its reach extending nationwide. Savills provides a full range of property solutions enabling us to deliver market leading advice to help fulfil our Clients needs. Our broad range of specialist advisory, property management and transactional services that we provide benefit from the synergy and connectivity of our specialist departments.

33 Margaret Street,
London W1G 0JD
0207 409 8147
rcrook@savills.com
www.savills.co.uk

PROFILES

Visual Partner:

HayesDavidson

Celebrating its 25th year, London based Hayes Davidson LLP specialises in the visualisation of architecture and the built environment for planning and marketing. The highly experienced team helps clients achieve planning permission, raise funding, win competitions and gain press coverage. The Partnership has projects in the UK, Europe, China, New York, Miami and Hawaii. London projects include The Shard, King's Cross, BBC, Bloomberg, One Hyde Park, Earls Court and the Tate Modern.

Studio A,
21 Conduit Place,
London W2 1HS
020 7262 4100
www.hayesdavidson.com
@hayesdavidson

With thanks to:

LONDON METROPOLITAN ARCHIVES

London Metropolitan Archives (LMA) is home to an extraordinary range of documents, images, maps, films and books about London. It is the largest local authority record office in the United Kingdom, providing access to 105 km of archives – an enormous amount of information on London and Londoners. This material dates from 1067 to the present day and covers every imaginable subject. Collections which cover the development of London's estates are particularly strong, especially those of the London County Council, Greater London Council and City of London Corporation for the 20th century.

Offering a wide selection of talks, guided tours, film screenings, exhibitions and other events, LMA is free to use and open to everyone. Whether you're tracing your family history or researching any aspect of the capital's history, if you're interested in London or Londoners, LMA is the place to visit.

40 Northampton Road,
London EC1R 0HB
020 7332 3820
www.cityoflondon.gov.uk/lma

nla LONDON'S CENTRE FOR THE BUILT ENVIRONMENT

This Insight Study is published by NLA, and is supported by a major exhibition 'London's Growing Up!' and tall buildings events programme, taking place from April to June 2014

Curator
Peter Murray

Assistant curator
Catherine Staniland

Exhibition co-ordinator
Jenine Hudson

Research and text
Denise Chevin
Andrew Pring

Design
Niten Patel

PR and communications
Caro Communications

NLA team:
Peter Murray (Chairman); Nick McKeogh (Chief executive); Debbie Whitfield (Director); Bill Young (Financial controller); Catherine Staniland (Programme director); Jessame Cronin (Programme manager); Lucie Murray (Programme co-ordinator); Jenine Hudson (Exhibition and awards co-ordinator); Claire Hopkins (Business development director); Anna Cassidy (Account director); Laura Bushby (Account manager); Sarah Johnson (Account director); Danielle Rowland (Events director); Lauren Bennett (Events manager); Michelle Haywood (Events and marketing manager); Molly Nicholson (Events and marketing co-ordinator)

NLA – London's Centre for the Built Environment was founded in 2005 to provide an independent information resource and a forum for discussion and debate about London's built environment for professionals, public and politicians. Since that time it has successfully established itself as a major focus for discussion about architecture, planning, development and construction in the capital with a year–round programme of events, publications and exhibitions, and a core mission – bringing people and ideas together to shape a better city. www.newlondonarchitecture.org

INDEX

A

Abercrombie Plan, 1944 – 37
The Accidental Skyline – 104
Acton – 101
Adelaide House – 37
AECOM – 18, 20
Alban Gate – 45
Albert Embankment – 71
200 Aldersgate – 45
Aldgate – 26, 92
Aldgate Place – 92
Alexandra Palace – 22, 23
Allford Hall Monaghan Morris (AHMM) – 80, 98
Allies and Morrison – 86, 92, 95, 100
Areas of Intensification – 21
Aukett Fitzroy Robinson – 99
The Aviva Tower (see also Commercial Union building) – 41, 104

B

Balfron Tower – 38, 39
Banglatown – 103
Bank of England – 44
Bankside – 26, 27
Barbican Centre – 24, 38, 39, 40, 67
Barclays – 18
Barker, Nigel – 30
Barnet Council – 100
Battersea Power Station – 71
BBC – 99
Bennetts Associates Architects – 94
Berkeley – 90, 92, 94, 96
Big Ben - 27
Bishopsgate – 18, 22, 48, 92
Bishopsgate Goodsyard – 92, 103
Blackfriars Mile – 80
Blackfriars Road – 27, 80
240 Blackfriars – 80, 81
Blackfriars Station – 80

Blackheath Point – 22, 23
The Boomerang (see One Blackfriars) – 80
Borough – 26, 27
Brent – 100, 101
Brent Cross Cricklewood – 100
Brent Cross Main Square – 100
Brent Cross Shopping Centre – 100
Brick Lane – 103
British Land – 49, 92
British Waterways – 94
Broadgate Estate – 49
Broadgate Tower – 49, 67
55 Broadway – 37
Broadway Chambers – 95
Broadway Malyan – 49, 71, 77
Brutalist – 37
Buckingham Palace – 40
Building a Better London – 50
Building for the 21st Century – 33
Buro Happold – 27
BXC Development Partners – 100

C

25 Cabot Square – 45
Camden – 58
Canada Water - 27
261 Canal Road – 94
Canaletto – 94
Canary Wharf – 24, 44, 45, 46, 48, 49, 52, 86, 104
Canary Wharf Group – 19, 32, 84, 86
Canning Town – 39
The Carlyle Group – 80
Cathy Come Home – 41
Central Activity Zone (CAZ) – 05, 16, 21
Central Park – 47
Centre Point – 40, 41, 43, 67
Chalegrove Properties – 90
Chamberlin, Powell and Bon – 37, 38, 40

The Cheesegrater (see The Leadenhall Building) – 48
Chelsea Barracks – 33
Chelsfield – 27, 84
Chicago – 45
China - 18
Chinese investment – 71
The Chrysler Building – 104
City Forum – 94
City Hall – 22
City of London – 13, 14, 18, 21, 24, 25, 26, 40, 45, 47, 48, 49, 50, 55, 80, 104, 106
City of Westminster – 27
City Pride – 55, 90
City Road Basin – 94
250 City Road – 94
Civil Aviation Authority (CAA) – 24
Columbus Tower – 55
Commission for Architecture and the Built Environment (CABE) – 17, 20, 22, 24, 28, 30, 48, 50, 103, 104
Commercial Union building (see also Aviva Tower) – 41, 104
Conservation Areas – 21, 27, 47
Convoys Wharf – 96
Cossons, Sir Neil – 13
Council on Tall Buildings and Urban Habitat (CTBUH) – 19
County of London Development Plan, 1951 – 37
Create Streets – 18
Create Streets: Not just multi-storey estates – 18
Credit Suisse First Boston – 45
Cripplegate – 37, 40
Crossrail – 96, 101
Croydon – 98
Cruickshank, Dan – 103

118 LONDON'S GROWING UP!

D

Dalian Wanda Group – 71, 77
Darbourne and Darke – 17
David Chipperfield Architects – 27, 84
Davis, Robert – 27
Densification – 13
Density – 05, 16, 17, 18, 47, 58, 71, 86, 101, 104
Department for Culture, Media and Sport (DCMS) – 30
Deptford – 96
Deptford Creek – 96
Design Council – 17
Docklands – 104
Doon Street – 84, 85
Dorrington – 104
Draft Further Amendments to the London Plan, 2014 – 20
Draft London Plan (2002) – 17
Dubai – 13

E

Eagle House – 92
Ealing – 58, 101
Earls Court – 99
The eastern cluster – 26, 104
Eastern fringe – 26
The East End Preservation Society – 103
The Economist Building – 40, 42
Elephant and Castle – 21, 27, 78, 80
Elephant and Castle Supplementary Planning Guidance – 78
Elizabeth House – 27, 84
Eileen House – 21, 78
Emberton Joseph – 44
The Empire State Building – 48, 104
Empress State Building – 40, 99
England – 18
English Heritage – 13, 20, 22, 24, 28, 30, 48, 71, 84, 103, 104

Enterprise Zone – 45
Ernö Goldfinger – 38, 39

F

Farrell, Terry – 96
Farrells – 45, 92, 96
20 Fenchurch Street – 13, 32, 67
Fenchurch Street Station – 26
Fire Brigade – 37
Foster + Partners – 47, 48, 90, 92, 94, 103

G

G Ware Travelstead – 45
General Wolfe statue – 22
Georgian – 17
Georgian Group – 17
Gerald Robson – 48
The Gherkin (see 30 St Mary Axe) – 13, 24, 48, 50, 64, 77
GL Hearn – 05, 55-63
Glasshouse Gardens – 95
Golden Lane Estate – 37, 40
Gollins Melvin Ward (GMW) – 41
Goodman's Field – 92
The Goodsyard – 92
The Government – 28, 34, 50
Grand Union Canal – 101
Great Arthur House – 37, 39
The Great Fire – 104
Great Maze Pond – 28
Great Ropemaker Partnership – 80, 81
Greater London Authority (GLA) – 13, 16, 17, 21, 22, 28, 47, 48, 96, 101, 104
Greater London Council (GLC) – 37
Green Belt – 17, 21, 103
Greenwich – 20, 58, 96
Greenwich Park – 22
Greenwich Peninsula – 96
Greenwich Riverside – 96

Greycoat – 41
Groveworld – 94
Guidance on Tall Buildings – 20
Guy's Hospital – 28

H

Hackney Council – 39
Hammersmith and Fulham – 99, 101
Hammerson – 100
Hampstead – 50
Harlesden – 101
Hayes Davidson – 14, 19, 31, 35, 68, 73, 75, 82, 88, 107
Haymarket – 42
The Heaney case – 32
The Heron Tower – 22, 28, 48, 50, 67
Herzog & de Meuron – 19, 86
Hilton Hotel – 27
Historic Royal Palaces – 22
Hong Kong – 90
Hounslow – 58
Housing Forum – 13
HS2 (High Speed 2) – 101
Hungerford Bridge – 71
Hutchison Whampoa – 96
Hyams, Harry – 40
Hyde Park – 47

I

Ian Simpson Architects – 80
iCity – 95
Imperial College – 99
Imperial West – 99
The International Quarter – 95
Ipsus Mori – 63-67
Isle of Dogs – 45, 47, 90
Islington – 18, 94

INDEX

J

Jenkins, Simon – 103
Johnson, Boris – 50, 96
Joiner Street – 28
Jubilee Line – 46

K

Kensington and Chelsea – 99
Kensington Barracks – 27
Kenwood House – 22
Kew – 20, 30
King Henry VIII's Mound – 22
King's Reach Tower – 26
Knight Frank – 19
Kohn Pederson Fox Associates (KPF) – 19, 26, 48, 77

L

La Défense – 104
Lambeth – 58, 71
Lambeth Bridge – 71
The Lambeth Core Strategy – 13
Lambeth Council – 27, 84
Land Securities – 32
Larsen-Nielsen system – 39
Lawrence, Andrew – 18
Le Corbusier – 37
Leadenhall Market – 26
Leadenhall Street – 41
Lend Lease – 78, 95
Lewisham – 96
Lewisham Council – 96
Lexicon Tower – 94
Liebowitz, Alan – 103
Lifschutz Davidson Sandilands – 84, 92
Lillie Road – 40
Lillington Garden Estate – 17
Lister, Sir Edward - 103
Liverpool Street Station - 26

Livingstone, Ken – 28, 47, 50
Localism Act, 2011 – 34
54 Lombard Street – 45
360 London (see Newington Butts)
London Bridge – 17, 26, 27, 28, 49, 71
London Building Act – 37
London & Continental Railways - 95
London City Airport – 46
London County Council (LCC) – 37, 40
London Docklands Development Corporation – 45
London High – 44
London Millennium tower – 47
London Plan – 17, 18, 20, 24, 47, 90, 100, 101
London School of Economics (LSE) – 13, 104
London South Central – 27
London View Management Framework (LVMF) – 22, 23, 71
London Wall – 40, 42, 45
Loughborough University – 95
LSE Cities – 104
Ludgate and Sampson House – 80
Luftwaffe – 45

M

Manhattan – 47
Manhattan Loft Corporation – 95
Manhattan Loft Gardens – 95
Mansion House – 44
Mappin & Webb – 44
Maritime Greenwich – 20, 30
Marsh Wall – 90
The Mayor – 05, 13, 17, 20, 21, 22, 24, 28, 50, 78, 96, 100, 106
Metropolitan Open Land – 21
Millbank Tower – 40
Miller Development – 94
Ministry of Sound – 78
Minster Court – 45

Mixed-use – 17, 19, 33, 86, 92, 95, 98, 101
Modern Movement – 37, 45
Modernism – 40
The Municipal Arts Society – 104

N

National Housing Federation – 17
National Planning Policy Framework (NPPF) - 28
The National Theatre – 84
The National Trust – 103
National Westminster Tower (NatWest Tower) (see also Tower 42) – 41, 44, 67
Neighbourhood Plans – 34
New Cross – 96
New Oxford Street – 41
New York – 104
New Zealand House – 40, 42
Newham Department of Planning and Architecture – 38
Newington Butts – 78, 79
Nine Elms – 71 - 77
No 1 Croydon – 98
North Circular Road – 100
25 North Colonnade – 45
North Kensington – 38, 39
Northern Line – 71

O

The O2 Arena – 96
Oakmaye Properties – 78
Old Broad Street – 44
Old Oak Common – 101
Old Street – 92, 94
Old Street roundabout – 94
Olympia & York – 45, 47
2012 Olympic Games – 95
Olympic Park – 95
Olympicopolis – 95

One Blackfriars – 80, 81
One Cabot Square – 45
One Canada Square – 45
One Nine Elms – 71, 77
One St George Wharf (see The Tower)
One the Elephant – 78
Opportunity Area – 20, 21, 58, 63, 71, 78, 90, 99, 100, 103, 104
Opportunity Area Planning Framework (OAPF) – 71, 103, 104
Outstanding Universal Value – 30
Ove Arup – 39
Oxford Street – 40

P

P & O Building – 41
Paddington – 27
Palace of Westminster – 20, 22, 30, 31, 50, 71, 84
Palumbo, Peter – 44
Paolozzi, Eduardo – 40
Park Avenue – 104
Parker Morris – 17
Parliament Hill – 22, 68
Parliamentary Select Committee for Transport, Local Government and the Regions – 17
Paris – 17, 104, 106
Pelli, Cesar – 45, 46
Pembroke Real Estate – 94
Peninsula Quay – 96
Piano, Renzo – 24, 49, 50, 51, 103
Pimlico – 17
Planning system – 05, 13, 20, 21, 22, 24, 26, 28, 30, 32, 33, 34, 36, 44, 47, 50, 58, 63, 84, 96, 103, 104
PLP Architecture – 80, 81, 99
The Pinnacle – 18, 19, 48, 55, 104
Pompidou Centre – 49
Poplar – 38
Portland House – 40, 42

Post Modern – 45
Prescott, John – 22, 48, 71
Primrose Hill – 22
Prince Charles (see also the Prince of Wales) – 33, 45
Principle Place – 92
Pringle Brandon Perkins+Will – 92
Public realm – 21, 28, 33, 80, 87, 90, 92

Q

Qatari Diar – 84
Qataris – 33
Quay House – 55
Queens Park Rangers – 101
The Queen's Walk – 22

R

Rafael Viñoly Architects – 32
Recession – 46
Rees, Peter – 28
Regeneration – 21, 27, 47, 50, 58, 71, 78, 80, 92, 96, 101, 104
Regent's Canal – 94
Richmond Park – 22
Right to light – 31 - 33
River Brent – 100
Robertson, Howard Sir – 42
Robbins, Peter – 27
Rogers, Richard – 17, 49
Rogers Stirk Harbour + Partners (RSHp) – 78, 79, 86
Rolfe Judd Architects – 71, 98
Ronan Point – 38, 39
The Royal Arsenal Riverside – 96
Royal Botanic Gardens – 20, 30
Royal College of Art – 13
Royal family – 40
Royal Parks – 27
Royal Parks Foundation – 24
Russell Square – 37

S

Saffron Square – 98
Sainsbury's Nine Ems – 71
Savills – 18
Second World War – 37, 39, 40
The Secretary of State – 22, 24
Section 106 – 28, 47, 80, 104
Seifert, Richard – 40, 41, 44, 98
Sellar, Irvine – 49
Sellar – 28, 49, 50
Senate House – 37
The Serpentine – 22
Shadows – 33
Shanghai – 13
Shangri-La Hotel – 49
The Shell Centre – 24, 31, 40, 42, 84
Shoreditch – 92, 103
Shoreditch High Street – 92
Skyline – 05, 13, 21, 28, 33, 47, 50, 55, 71, 78, 80, 90, 100, 103, 105, 106
Slums – 37, 38
Smithson, Alison and Peter – 42
SOM (Skidmore, Owings & Merrill) – 45, 46, 94, 95, 104
South Quay – 18, 90
South Quay Plaza – 55
Southwark – 21, 26, 27, 28, 58, 78, 80
Southwark Council – 21, 27, 28, 50, 78, 80
Square Mile – 24, 32, 49
Squire and Partners – 78, 84, 90, 91
St George – 77
St George's Circus – 80
St James – 40
St Margaret's Church – 30
St Paul's Cathedral – 22, 23, 25, 26, 37, 44, 48, 49, 50
St Paul's Heights – 26
St Thomas Street - 28
Stadium Capital Developments – 101
The Stage – 92

121

INDEX

Standard Life Investments – 100
Stanton Williams – 86
Star architects – 50
Stirling Wilford – 45
Stone, Toms & Partners – 40
Strata Tower – 67, 78, 79
Strategic Tall Building Research Paper, 2010 – 26
Stratford – 95
Stratford Plaza – 95
Swiss Re – 48
Supplementary Planning Document (SPD) – 27, 78, 80
Swanke Hayden Connell Architects – 96

T

Taylor Woodrow-Anglian – 39
Tall Towers 2012 – 19
Telford Homes – 95
TfL – 71
Thatcher, Margaret – 45
The Can of Ham (60 St Mary Axe) – 48
The Gherkin (30 St Mary Axe) – 13, 24, 48, 50, 64
The Helter Skelter (see also The Pinnacle) – 48
The Leadenhall Building – 13, 48, 49, 50, 67, 104
The Thames river – 13, 18, 21, 22, 26, 80, 96
The Tower – 71, 77
The Tower of London – 20, 22
The Shard – 13, 18, 22, 24, 26, 28, 49, 50, 64, 67, 80, 103
The Skyscraper Index – 18
The Stump (see The Pinnacle) – 48
The Walkie Talkie (see also 20 Fenchurch Street) – 24
Tottenham Court Road – 27, 40
Towards An Urban Renaissance – 17
Tower 42 (see also National Westminster Tower) – 41, 44, 67
Tower Hamlets – 18, 63, 90
Tower Hamlets Council – 86, 90
Tourists – 50
Travers, Professor Tony – 13, 17
Trellick Tower – 38, 39

U

UBM – 80
United Nations Educational, Scientific and Cultural Organisation (UNESCO) – 30, 31
University College London – 95
UNStudio – 94
Urban Task Force report (1998) – 17

V

Van der Rohe, Mies – 44
Vancouver – 90, 104
Vancouverism – 104
Vauxhall – 17, 71 - 77, 104, 106
Vauxhall Gyratory – 71
Vauxhall Tube station – 71
Vauxhall Tower (see The Tower)
Vauxhall Nine Elms – 71 - 77
Victoria – 27, 42
Victoria & Albert Museum – 95
Viewing corridors – 22, 50
2020 Vision – 13
Von Clemm, Michael – 45

W

Wales – 18
The Walkie Talkie (see 20 Fenchurch Street)
Wall Street on Water – 45
Wandsworth – 58, 71
Wandsworth Council – 71
Waterloo – 24, 27, 31, 71, 82, 84
Waterloo Bridge – 22, 76, 80, 82, 84
Waterloo Station – 84
Wates – 39
West 57th Street – 104
West Brompton – 39
West Kensington – 99
Westfield – 99
Westminster Abbey – 20, 30
Westway – 99
White City Opportunity Area – 99
The White Tower – 22
Wood Wharf – 18, 86, 87
Woolwich – 96
World Heritage Convention – 30
World Heritage Sites – 27, 28, 30, 31
Wright, Herbert – 44

X

-

Y

York Road – 84

Z

Zone d'Action Concert (ZAC) – 104